Beyond Central,
Toward Acceptance

Beyond Central, Toward Acceptance

A Collection of Oral Histories
From Students of Little Rock Central High

BUTLER
CENTER

BOOKS

Little Rock, Arkansas

BUTLER
CENTER

BOOKS

The Butler Center for Arkansas Studies
Central Arkansas Library System
100 Rock Street
Little Rock, Arkansas 72201
Butlercenterbooks.org

Little Rock Central High School
1500 South Park Street
Little Rock, Arkansas 72202
www.lrchmemory.org

ISBN 978-1-935106-21-0
10-digit ISBN 1-935106-21-X

Cover illustration: Shariq Ali
Cover design: Mackie O'Hara
Book design: H. K. Stewart

Printed in the United States of America

This book is printed on archival-quality paper that meets requirements of the American National Standard for Information Sciences, Permanence of Paper, Printed Library Materials, ANSI Z39.48-1984.

This book is dedicated to the Little Rock Nine,

whose courage turned the doors of Central High

into gates of change for America,

and to all the Memory Project interviewees,

whose stories of this change have become

lifelong lessons for our students.

The Memory Project Revolving Loan Fund

Special Thanks to
the teachers, staff, administration and
Parent Teacher Student Association of Little Rock Central High School
for their generous help in establishing the
Memory Project Revolving Loan Fund.

All proceeds generated by the sale of this book will be added to this permanent fund. The fund exists to support future student research, publications, and interpretive works documenting the oral history of civil rights, teaching tolerance, promoting acceptance, fostering unity in the community, and building personal relationships enriched by equity and diversity.

These projects honor Central High's legacy as a turning point in the struggle for civil rights both in our community and the nation and also acknowledge our obligations—and our opportunities—to wear the mantle of change in positive ways in the future.

The goal of the *Memory Project Revolving Loan Fund* is to open a door into history and encourage students today to continue the process of change in race relations and civil rights in their own lives and communities.

Second Edition Printing

This second edition of Beyond Central, Toward Acceptance *has been supported with funding from the* **Memory Project Revolving Loan Fund** *and a matching grant from* **Learn and Serve America***, a project of the Corporation for National & Community Service and the Arkansas Department of Education.*

Contents

Teachers' Preface

Turning history over to the next generation requires trust. It also involves more than a little anxiety. The teachers sponsoring this book project all agree on this. But we also have agreed—from the beginning and repeatedly throughout the project—to let our students decide what belongs in this book.

The idea for this book sprouted soon after we read the first batch of interview essays written by our 9th grade Civics students in year one of the *Memory Project* here at Central. We had not been sure that high school freshmen knew enough history to write about the history they heard in those conversations with older family members. We expected a lot to be lost in translation between the spoken word and the written account, especially with such young writers and such distant history. Instead, we found that 15-year olds—although they may miss the history behind some detail mentioned in passing—do have a keen ear for stories about experiences that change a person. They respond to the power of personal stories, and many intuitively used the power of storytelling when they retold the stories they heard. And their *Memory Project* essays captured the experiences their older relatives saw and felt during times of civil rights struggles and the changes they went through in attitude and relationships with people of different racial and ethnic background.

These students' *Memory Project* essays, we decided, were a bumper crop for historians. Not only were students digging up oral history about desegregation at Central High and elsewhere from many individuals with multiple points of view, they were depositing another layer of history. When they picked for their essay the "one story in particular that stayed with me from this interview," the students were giving us, an older generation, the chance to learn what they found important in our stories about our lessons from history.

As teachers at Central, we decided that we could learn still more if we let our students become the historians. This time we invited current students at Central to publish a book of selected essays from the

Memory Project. The students' task was to tell us "which of these essays are especially important for others to read." But, as we started out saying, turning over history to the next generation involves both trust and trepidation.

One fear for us teachers is that all of the things we consider important will not make the cut. Students today may not notice a fleeting reference to some historical detail that we older adults link to something significant. Young students may also overlook some deeper truth about human relations and personal choice that we adults find buried in a story.

There's still another fear we have in leaving "the history" to our students: we leave them vulnerable to historians with special agendas. Scholars, eyewitnesses and other groups often have a vested interest in their interpretations of events. Student historians who do not voice the same thesis can be criticized quickly. During the 50th commemoration of Central's desegregation, there was considerable public debate—and disagreement—by supporters of competing versions of historical events. And, as current headlines remind us, our racial history in America can still be a minefield in this regard.

Yet for all these dangers, we as teachers think it is both appropriate and necessary for our students to take charge of this book. As adults, we've had our chance to decide which part of the oral history of civil rights is important for others to learn. Now it's their turn.

And, we stand by the work these students have begun. Regardless of lessons of history we might think they have missed, it is very evident to us that they have uncovered many important ones.

They have chosen essays showing us that the Crisis of '57 did not end on September 25th with a single executive order from the President. Several of the essays selected for the book detail the harassment and the isolation experienced by the Little Rock Nine throughout the long year. Other essays document the same struggle repeating in one school after another. Still others show the consequences, for both black and white students, when integration took place *without* careful guidance from school or community leaders.

The students also have designated a whole chapter for stories that describe how the Jim Crow code of laws, passed from the 1880s through the 1950s, separated black and white citizens in virtually every aspect of daily life. They have also pulled together essays showing us that the great divide of discrimination is not limited to race and does not stop at the borders of our region or our nation.

Moreover, these students-turned-historians give us essays that show the price paid by individuals—and by their communities—when discrimination of any kind is *not* confronted. And to their real credit, they recognized stories that went beyond just descriptions of the discrimination. The students have also identified essays that tell us how individuals tried to change the problems they saw. They show us oral histories that offer both inspiration and a blueprint for actions that others today can follow.

The book of history this team of students has compiled comes from a considerable amount of time and effort. They have met, voluntarily and daily, after school for anywhere from 30 minutes to an hour and a half; and they have done this for four months. Students volunteering for the reading team have each read a minimum of 30 essays; all members of the editing team read at least 100. Plus, when the team has disagreed on which essays to include or how to organize essays into chapters, they have talked with each other. Even when the discussions focused on current issues of racism or bias and discrimination, they have been willing to discuss their disagreements, instead of retreating figuratively to separate corners and to silent judgment. Many adults do not accomplish such a dialogue; we commend our students for beginning the conversation.

And, finally, we appreciate these student historians for finding a way to pull others into the hard but essential task of facing our history. Like good historians, the editing team has concluded their book with a list of questions for further study. They have given this next assignment to themselves and to their Central classmates, and they also give it to you, the readers of this book. ... Our students can become our teachers if we pay attention to what strikes them as important. This collection of Memory Project essays is an excellent place to tune in.

Memory Project Sponsors
George West, Keith Richardson, Cynthia Nunnley
June 2009

Editors' Foreword

The Memory Project began in 2004 in the Civics classes of Little Rock Central High to encourage incoming students to learn more about the historic events at the school 50 years earlier. As an assignment, students were asked to conduct an interview with someone who witnessed the Civil Rights Movement or experienced some form of discrimination. They were then asked to write an essay telling about the interview and what made the story they heard important for others to read. The essays they wrote were then posted onto a permanent website by the original Memory Project Team, a group that has now graduated. (For the curious, there's a link to copies of the lesson plans on the website: www.lrchmemory.org.)

The original team worked quite a bit on the website. They decided to create a Wiki, since the software allows new essays to be continuously added and easy access to related essays and topics. The team thought it was important to make this a student-created and student-run website. Even though some essays inevitably ended up with typos and indexing mistakes, either by the writer or by the students who volunteer to post the essays, the essays still represent the work and the thinking of students. In 2007, the 50th anniversary of the desegregation of Central, the project won a national award from the American Historical Association.

The next step in the project has been the creation of this book. Our goal after the book is to create a template based on the website so that others can create similar oral history projects.

The process of producing this book has been something of a voyage of discovery, this being our first time to design and edit and actually make a book. In early 2009, the first call went out for editors and readers and we began assembling after school. The assignment for volunteer readers was one pair of questions: "Which of the Memory Project essays is especially important for others to read, and why?"

At that point, the meetings were mostly discussion. The book seemed very far away, and without a group of essays to work with, there wasn't much to do besides discuss. We created a ranking system and made a few early decisions about how the content of the book, especially the essays, would be presented. The less intrusion, the better—we wanted to keep the essays as close as possible to how the students wrote them. We would edit for clarity only, leaving quoted material alone and assuming that the student had recorded the quote correctly.

The reading process was scattershot. We basically handed everyone who showed up a list of 20-30 essays on the Project website, told them to get back to us with their comments, and we'd sort it out. That didn't work out as well as we'd hoped. Not all essays were reviewed, much less by three different readers as planned. Some essays that definitely merited inclusion were overlooked but were discovered toward the end, fortunately, and included.

That was the first stage. The second stage was more systematic because the second stage involved computers and spreadsheets. We had readers score the essays 0-2 in terms of whether to include it in the book, where 2 meant "Yes" and 1 meant "Maybe." Using the wonderful power of Microsoft Excel, the editing team could easily concentrate on the 1s and 2s and make decisions about whether the essay would be included or not. (We have more to say in the conclusion about how those decisions helped us define exactly what *does* make an essay important for others to read.)

After that, there were two issues to work with: creating a spreadsheet of information for use in the index and editing hard copies of the essays.

This editing part of the process had some mistakes, too, because any bunch of high school students, even a bunch with the fancy title of "editors" has a somewhat limited knowledge of the intricacies of grammar. The problem of grammatical errors in the essays seemed easy to answer at first: fix them. But then we thought about the other kind of information that can come from grammar: namely, the author's voice and the dialogue between the student and the person they were interviewing. Grammatical mistakes aren't necessarily a part of a writer's voice but are often some faulty construction or a student reaching for words that they might not really know when they were trying to explain what they heard. It seemed more authentic to leave essays as close to the way they were first written, and we especially wanted to keep the writer's voice apparent to the reader.

Clarity became the defining word in the discussion. We would edit for clarity, but nothing else. We were willing to add commas, use parentheses, and change prepositions where necessary but only to make a sentence clear.

We also thought about how to handle derogatory terms and language used in the passages and left them as the writer wrote them. Profanity, racial slurs, and demonyms like "African American" and "Caucasian" were kept exactly as they appeared in the original essay, because the use of the word by the author often mirrors the tone of the essay itself. There was no way to alter that strategy of the author, and we had no desire to do so.

Other than these changes, we kept the essays in the same form the author wrote them with one more exception: you'll notice if you visit the website that a number of early essays have a paragraph at the end with an "Author's Note." Normally, this was filled with advice for ninth graders doing the essays in the future. This is the only part of any essay that we cut out entirely (and then only if the note was unrelated to the central story in the essay).

After having all the essays selected and edited, the next problem was the organization. We didn't start with a title for the book or with any ideas for the chapter names within the book. We struggled, trying to make these decisions.

At first we thought we would group the essays by the race of the narrator, which is one of the categories the original Memory Project Team set up for the website. But then we recognized that it would skew thought about the book and make it seem focused exclusively on racial discrimination. The more essays we all read, the more we agreed that the stories in the essays went beyond the events at Central and beyond race, too. We had something resembling our current system in the works when Cameron Zohoori, a member of the original team, paid a surprise visit from college and helped create the system of organization we finally put in place.

The system, you'll notice, follows our thinking process. It starts, to be honest..., from a narrow perspective. Our first chapter,

"Central," focuses on the crisis at Central High. Zooming out, we have "Beyond Central," which is about the desegregation stories of other schools in Arkansas and elsewhere. Zooming out even more, we have "Beyond Schools," which focuses on stories from many other life settings where segregation was legally enforced. From there, the book pans to "Beyond Race and Borders," which contains essays about discrimination on a basis other than race or discrimination that took place outside of the country. Finally we have "Toward Acceptance," which deals with stories about individual activism and personal efforts to end segregation and discrimination.

After we created the divisions for chapters, the issue of how to arrange the essays within them became an issue. We discussed how we should sequence them. We decided on multiple schemes for different chapters. In "Central," with the narrative of a single event binding the stories, sorting them based on building tension was feasible. In "Beyond Central" we sequenced them based on which state the action occurred in. In "Beyond Schools," grouping them based on where the discrimination occurred helps show how omnipresent Jim Crow was and how discrimination still exists. We sorted based on country and cause of discrimination in "Beyond Race and Borders." These stories happened in different places, in different times, and to different people. In "Toward Acceptance" we sequenced the essays so the stories of activism went toward positive change and not only altering the status quo. Showing the maturity of the activism demonstrated was an excellent way to build this chapter.

For all the details about process that we the readers and editors used to put this book together, however, this book isn't about us. It's about the experiences that older family members and friends have shared with students, about the history that the students were able to come in contact with, and about the essays that young ninth grade writers have put on paper to try to pass on the stories they heard. This was a valuable learning experience for the student authors and for the readers and editors of the essays.

Now, turn the page and let the stories happen for you, too.

The Central High Memory Project Editing Team
May 2009

Chapter One:
Central

Central High—Front View
Jennifer Perren

Editors' Commentary

Most people with background knowledge of United States history know the textbook version of the Central High Integration Crisis: there were nine African American students who were turned away from the doors of the school by an angry mob and the Arkansas National Guard, who had been called by the governor. Yet most do not know about the stories and experiences of the individual people involved or how they dealt with the crisis and the change. In 1957, as the world was watching Little Rock, the citizens of Little Rock had their lives dramatically changed, whether they chose to act as passive observers of history or active supporters of integration or segregation.

This conflict was where it all began, where the seed of this book was planted. This chapter is especially important because it sets up the foundation for the rest of the book; it opens a portal to what really went on in Central High when the crisis occurred; and, it gives the reader a true reflection of the events to understand why it was, and still is, an important issue to the world and those people involved.

Like every great conflict, there were those people who were directly involved and those people who witnessed the crisis. This chapter consists of stories from both viewpoints during and after the crisis. Despite all of the trouble they went through, Spirit Trickey claims that the Little Rock Nine never regretted what they did; they just hoped for the world to learn and continue to grow in acceptance. After 1957, the problems didn't end for the students in Little Rock. After the end of the 1957 school year, the Lost Year began, when all of the city's high schools were shut down by Orval Faubus. During that time, Daisha Booth's grandmother, Rose Booth, explained that many African American children were moved to her rural, all-black high school, which caused overcrowding and other conflicts. When the schools reopened Fall 1959, Dr. Sybil J. Hampton began attending Little Rock Central and became the first African American to complete all three years of high school and graduate from Central. Emily Dobson conducted the interview and thus continued the story of the struggles presented during integration. Even 25 years after the crisis, Karen Lovelace testified that, as an African American student, she didn't feel fully welcomed at Central and that racial typecasting existed even in the drama department.

Ja'Nena Shelton's essay gives the reader a brief overview of the Little Rock Central High crisis. Her great aunt was one of Carlotta Walls' good friends and spent hours talking to Carlotta on the phone during the crisis. It's a fascinating perspective that isn't presented very often in any history text, and it serves as a good example of the untold histories we hope to bring to the surface through this project. Sara Goldsholl's reflective interview with a white student from Central recognizes the tension in the school during the conflict, and how some students took the initiative later to reconcile the injustices with the Little Rock Nine. Michelle McCain's interview with Ford Nelson revealed the unease that the crisis created around the country and how the people dealt with it. The way history books present the issue, it's easy to overlook how many people were affected personally by the struggle to integrate one school. While the stories of the Lost Year are now being documented, the efforts taken by citizens to get their schools back and to have them integrated finally are not nearly as well known as the events of 1957-58. Their efforts are being preserved in this book with the essays from Kristen Smith and Andrew Kurrus who interviewed some of the major players in the movement to reopen the schools. The first attempts came through the Women's Emergency Committee and ultimately through the S.T.O.P. Campaign (Stop This Outrageous Purge), which led a recall election to remove segregationists on the Little Rock school board who fired teachers and administrators who had supported the integration in the previous year. The stories of all the people involved in integration are imperative to truly understanding the process of successfully insuring equality.

One of the most surprising stories in this chapter, "Because of the Racism, I was Frightened to Go to America," is from an anonymous author who illustrates the lasting impact Central's news story had on his father, a North Vietnamese child. This essay shows just how far the Central headlines spread and how important singular events can be in forming opinions and stereotypes.

A Long Walk
Sophie King

She Knew What to Expect at Central

On Saturday December 16th, 2006, Dr. Sybil J. Hampton and I were seated in my living room. Comfortable in an arm chair, in a room decorated with portraits, original paintings, and books, Dr. Hampton jogged her memory and recalled her experiences as the first African-American student at Little Rock Central High to attend all three years at the school and graduate.

Dr. Hampton grew up in Little Rock. Her parents were active members of the NAACP, leaders in their church, and the owners of a grocery store for other African Americans living in their neighborhood. She was an active participant in the Girl Scout program, was engaged in the YMCA, and took ballet, tap,

Interviewer:
Emily Dobson

Interviewee:
Dr. Sybil
Hampton

Time Period:
1950s

Location:
Little Rock, AR

Affected Group:
African
American

Setting:
School

and piano lessons. She had a paper route with the Arkansas State Press, which was, at that time, owned by Daisy Bates. Also, Dr. Hampton frequently assisted her parents at their grocery store.

Dr. Hampton was the first African American to attend Little Rock Central High School for all three years and graduate. At that time, students attended Central from grades 10 through 12. Her parents, being self employed, did not run the risk of losing their jobs simply for sending their daughter to school, unlike other families. Four of the Little Rock Nine were active members of Dr. Hampton's church, so she knew what to expect at Central and was fully aware of the integration going on. She began at Central in the fall of 1959 as a sophomore. By agreeing to attend Central, Dr. Hampton sacrificed her right to participate in extracurricular activities.

Most memorable of all Dr. Hampton's stories of growing up in Little Rock during the time of integration were those telling of her experiences at Central High School. She recalled that she was shunned by the entire student population and was acknowledged only by the other five African American students also enrolled at Central. "The French exchange student that was here was the only Caucasian student who spoke to me in three years," she remembers. "As I walked through the hall, students would push themselves against the lockers... rather than act out toward me violently, they simply ignored my presence. I learned what it was to be truly invisible."

There was one specific story that has stuck in my mind. Every day, as Dr. Hampton was walking up the stairs to class, she would pass a mentally challenged boy who always stood outside his classroom. "Every day, he was the only one that looked at me, but he never smiled at me." One day, as she was passing his classroom, he spat right into her face. "No one around us looked in our direction. There was absolutely no reaction. I was still invisible to everyone but this boy," she remembers. Dr. Hampton was able to find comfort from one of the school secretaries, Ms. Huckabee. Ms. Huckabee helped her clean herself off and commented, "Sybil, now you're dealing with white trash."

Through this experience, Dr. Hampton learned the importance of kindness. "I learned how important it was to simply give people respect. Even if you don't know them, and don't talk to them, it means a lot just to smile and acknowledge that someone's there. My experiences at Central also helped me to learn how to be calm. This helped later in life, when I was in difficult situations or under a lot of pressure. Also, it helped me to become a great listener, and the importance of just letting someone talk. Not to mention, I learned great eavesdropping skills! With no one talking to me, and no one caring that I was around, I was able to hear all the good gossip and piece information together. This helped me learn how to pay attention and analyze situations without even being a part of them, a skill that has done me well."

Although her experiences at Central may not have exactly been the perfect example of typical liberty and justice that is promoted by America, they did lay the proper foundation for Dr. Hampton's future. She graduated in 1962 in the top quarter of her graduating class. She went on to attend Earlham College. She earned a B.A. in English, and then went on to teach at Iona College and University of

Wisconsin at Madison. She was able to further her education at Georgetown University, and later received her doctorate from Cambridge University. In 1996 she became the president of the Winthrop Rockefeller Foundation, a charity organization promoting the education and success of underprivileged people in Arkansas.

The stories I learned from Dr. Sybil J. Hampton drastically changed the way I view civil rights. It allowed me to get a good look at what was going on at Central High School during integration. Also, this interview helped me realize that the Civil Rights Movement was not simply about legal rights, but also deals a lot with the mind-set of people and how they act toward others. I learned that it is always important to treat someone with respect.

Through the Storm
"I Never Felt Oppressed"

For my interview about civil rights, I chose to interview my great aunt, Ruth. My aunt is 63 years old and knows a lot about civil rights, because of the simple fact that she was born into segregation and she witnessed a lot of discrimination. I interviewed her in my room over the phone because although she's 63, she is still on the go 24/7. As the interview took place, I learned a lot about my aunt and civil rights that I didn't even know. In this essay, you will be able to come on this journey with me and hopefully learn some new interesting things that you didn't know before.

When the interview first began, I asked Ruth to tell me a little bit of what she knew about the Little Rock Nine. She told me that she knew the Little Rock Nine personally. In fact, Carlotta Walls was one of her best friends. She informed me that she and Carlotta shared many phone conversations about what she was going through at Central.

I quote: "Me and Carlotta shared many phone conversations on the events that were taking place at Central. (pause) She told me that they were not able to participate in extra curricular activities such as band, cheerleading, student council, drill team—none of that. And she told me the white kids wouldn't talk to the black kids, and that she would often receive threatening phone calls. In fact, Carlotta and I had to stop talking on the phone at one point because the phone was barred, because of the phone calls."

Ruth told me that she had to be at least 14 years old and in the 10th grade, living on 3023 West 17th St. at the corner of 17th and Pine at the time. As she began to elaborate on the subject, she informed me that she was asked to go to Central along with many

Interviewer:	Ja'Nena Shelton
Interviewee:	Ruth Evelyn Gee Williams
Time Period:	1950s
Location:	Little Rock, AR
Affected Group:	African American
Setting:	School

other students but she turned the offer down because she had just
become the cheerleading captain at Horace Mann High and she knew
that she could not be "passive" toward some of the situations she
would most likely be in. When I asked her if she could remember any
particular events or experiences, she called out five to me.

The first event she recalled was the day that Elizabeth Eckford set
out on her way to Central by herself because she had not been
informed that the Nine were to meet up and go to Central together.
She recalled that Elizabeth stayed down the street from her, and she
remembered how sorry she felt for Elizabeth when she found out that
she had embarked on that [dangerous] journey all by herself.

The second day she recalled was the day Ernest Green graduated
from Central. She said it was a great victory and that she would never
forget that.

The third event she recalled was the year all the high schools in
Little Rock were closed. She said that blacks had to go anywhere possible. By anywhere she definitely meant anywhere. Some blacks were
able to move with relatives out of the city and even out of the state.
Some of her friends moved to California, Washington, and even
Chicago. But the ones that didn't have anywhere to go lied about
their age so that they could go into service. Ruth was one of the more
fortunate ones. She was able to attend J. C. Cook High in
Wrightsville, Arkansas. Although the blacks were going through these
hardships, the whites weren't as unfortunate.

This leads me into the fourth event that she recalled, the fact that
Governor Faubus opened a building and turned it into a whites-only
private school. The name of this school was T.J. Raney High School.
Today, it is a nursing home and is located between 16th and 17th on
Lewis St. Ruth felt that this was really unfair, but she marched on.

The fifth and final event that Ruth recalled is *The Class That
Should Have Been*. This was the class of 1958-1959 that was unable
to attend school because all high schools had been shut down. During
the interview, I asked Ruth if she remembered any particular things
people said or wrote.

She told me, "Well you know, I can't really think of anything in
particular, but there was one thing I do remember. I remember the

local media. They would exaggerate on the news so much. As a matter of fact, I remember my mom getting a phone call from some of my relatives from out of town, and they said, 'Girl, what is going on down there in Little Rock, are you all O.K.?'" Ruth told me that the media definitely stretched the truth a bit too far. Once we talked about everything concerning the Little Rock Nine, we began to touch more on the subject of civil rights and segregation.

In this part of the interview Ruth told me some of her experiences and encounters with segregation. The first thing I asked Ruth was if she actually witnessed the segregation of restaurants, bathrooms, stores, water fountains... etc. She informed me that she did.

Journey into the Civil Rights Movement

My name is Sara Goldsholl, and I interviewed Trudy Jacobson about the Civil Rights Movement. Trudy has been friends with my parents for years. Her daughter, Jana Cohen, has known my family since I was born, or even before. Trudy Jacobson had an amazing story to tell that really put an impact on my view of the integration of Central High School.

Although Trudy lived through a rough time, she had a pretty basic life. Her family was pretty well off. "I didn't need anything," admits Trudy. Her father owned and managed a lumber yard, therefore they were pretty wealthy. Trudy worked as a secretary for a judge at the Pulaski County Court House. She is now retired, at age 67. Trudy was born in Little Rock, Arkansas, and still lives there today.

Interviewer: Sara Goldsholl
Interviewee: Trudy Jacobson
Time Period: 1950s
Location: Little Rock, AR
Affected Group: African American
Setting: School

"We were just empty-headed teenagers in the 50s." Trudy was at Central High School the day the Little Rock Nine arrived for the first time, but she never really knew about the discrimination of black people in the 50s and 60s. She led an easy life, without problems amongst her family. Although she and the rest of her family were against the discrimination, she was never really in contact with black people. "The only time I saw them were when they worked in restaurants, worked in our yard, or when they did the house cleaning," says Trudy. Because Trudy never really saw violence or prejudice against black people, the arrival of the Little Rock Nine really opened her eyes to the real world. Trudy was a senior at Central, and back then, seniors had the opportunity to attend an extra class to help the staff in some manner. In this case, Trudy decided to work in the attendance office first block. On the day the Little Rock Nine walked into the school, some of the students' parents were telling them that if "those black kids" came to the school, they should be checked out. Trudy said, "Kids began lining up and practically crashing the walls down at the attendance office." Trudy was shocked enough already. "It was the most eye-opening experience of my life. Student had to explain why they were getting checked out on the check-out sheet. I could still see the page, they would write the word 'N-I-G-G-E-R-S.' They would write that as the reason they were leaving," Trudy describes, "It was just sheet after sheet. I couldn't believe people really felt that way." Trudy describes her story as an eye-opener. "It changed me for the rest of my life." This was probably the biggest story Trudy had to tell. She says that she personally never saw any abuse done to anybody. Considering Central is a huge school, it was probably almost impossible for her to see every single student in the school. However, Trudy had a French class with Melba Patillo, one of the Little Rock Nine. She never saw any abuse done to Melba, but she wishes she would have stood up for her. "I wished I had been more proactive," admits Trudy. At a Central reunion, she went up to Melba, and apologized for never doing something about the discrimination or standing up for her. She asked to give her a hug. "It was a very emotional experience for me," says Trudy. She declares that she is amazed at how the Little Rock Nine were able to go about at Central. "I can not imagine taking on that responsibility as a high school student," says Trudy while thinking about what it would be like to walk in the shoes of the Little Rock Nine. Trudy explains that the children back then had a very different lifestyle from children these days. "We didn't know we were in a crisis. Fear never entered our minds," explains Trudy. She says that her peers never really talked about the discrimination or the integration. "We just did our thing!" laughs Trudy. Trudy explains that when Hall High School opened, about 100 students of her class transferred. She said that most of the children left because of the integration. That means that one sixth of the senior class left Central High. However, Trudy thought that it was interesting since the students that left to attend Hall High School still came to the Central reunions. After Trudy graduated, she joined the Panel of American Women. "We were a group of women that were very diverse." They visited church groups, school groups, or whoever wanted to hear their stories. "It was the first time I've been equal with a black person," says Trudy. Although Trudy lived in a normal life with barely any problems, she had a different look on the events that happened at Central High School. She realized that there actually were problems back then, and that we should be so thankful that there is no more segregation. Trudy concludes that interview by stating, "There is still a lot wrong out there, but at least there are fully integrated schools."

If I learned anything from this experience, it is definitely that kids back then weren't aware of the social actions that we know about today. I would have expected every student at Central High School to be completely interested in the arrival of the Little Rock Nine. However, after talking to Trudy, I have noticed that kids back then were pretty oblivious to what was happening to our city. I actually think it is pretty sad that children back then didn't have the opportunity to learn about what was happening, especially when they were part of it. I feel like every person has the right to stand up for what they believe in, and I'm sure a lot of the students at Central held back what they wanted to do or say. My interview really affected my relationship with her. I didn't know Trudy very well at first. I mean, of course, I had known her for my entire life, but I never had a deep conversation with her. I respect her a lot more, and look up to her just because she has seen what discrimination is, and I think that many people don't understand how prejudiced people were back in the 50s and 60s, and how sad that time was. Although Trudy had a pretty simple life, she still knows how it felt to see people feel so strongly against one group of innocent people. When I think about my learning experience from this, it almost makes me sad. I feel this way because children should have known what they were supporting or opposing, and they never really got the opportunity. Anyhow, I'm very pleased that I was able to have a deep conversation with someone I've known for so long. I will always look to her as a role model from now on. Although she had a sad story to tell, knowing this story is inspiring and helps me trust that I can stand up for what I believe in.

It Was a Hard Time for Everyone

The room was small with a very hot fire in the fireplace. The house smelled thick with cigars. Mr. Schultz looked very comfortable in his own house in a room where he probably spends most of his time.

Mr. Schultz is an aging man who had a lot of information to give on the Little Rock Crisis. Mr. Bob grew up in Pine Bluff, Arkansas, with his family. He is now married to Mrs. Barbara Schultz who has already been interviewed for the Memory Project. She had a major role in the Women's Emergency Committee (WEC).

Mr. Schultz has worked as a lawyer for many years. At the time of the crisis he started a group for lawyers to support the S.T.O.P campaign. He had a lot to do with the S.T.O.P campaign and was actually with the man who made up the name. The purpose of this interview was to get Mr. Schultz's experience down on paper so it can be used by historians later in time. He has already been quoted in a book about the happenings in Little Rock called *Breaking the Silence*. I was also trying to gain some information from him that I didn't already know about the subject. This was a good way to do that because he actually had a firsthand experience and the story has not been changed by other editor's opinions. During the interview we talked about what he generally remembered about the Little Rock Crisis and we also talked about the S.T.O.P campaign and a little bit of the "Lost Year." He had a lot of good information to share on all of these topics.

One story that stuck out in my mind was the one that he told about the naming of the S.T.O.P campaign. He was with two other men (whose names I can't recall at the moment) eating lunch downtown. One of the men brought up the topic of a "catchy" phrase for

Interviewer: Andrew Kurrus
Interviewee: Bob Schultz
Time Period: 1950s
Location: Little Rock, AR
Affected Group: African American
Setting: School

the campaign they were doing to stop the purge that was going on in the school board. They decided on the name Stop This Outrageous Purge which was later known as the S.T.O.P. campaign. He seemed to brighten up a little when telling this part of the story because it probably wasn't as sad for him as the rest.

I think this experience changed Mr. Bob Schultz in many ways over his life. He seemed a little down on the subject probably because it brought back bad memories that he is trying to forget. It is hard for me to tell exactly what aspects of his life were changed because I wasn't around to see how he acted before the crisis and how he acted after the crisis. One thing that can be assumed is that if something did indeed change him, then it has stuck with him for almost 50 years because, for as long as my family has known him, he has always respected people of all race, gender, and religion.

Mr. Schultz's story can be related to the bigger history of America's struggle for "liberty and justice for all" because he was fighting for the rights of other people. When the school board was firing teachers that were believed to be integrationists, he fought hard for the recall election. He is a lawyer so he fights for liberty and justice on a daily basis, but he did it especially hard on this occasion. Justice was not served until the people who were denying those nine students what they deserved were taken out of their positions.

This interview changed the way I think about the Little Rock Crisis because I can see how it left Mr. Bob Schultz. He is usually a pretty upbeat man, but when we started talking about this subject his overall mood changed. He mentioned that it was a very hard time, but overall good prevailed and that's why Little Rock Central is what it is today. It must have been a very sad time that is a very serious part of our history. One piece of advice that I would give a student doing their interview is to pay close attention. There are some very valuable pieces of information in these interviews and it should not be overlooked. These stories need to be told because the generation that experienced this incident is aging rapidly and we can't afford for this valuable piece of our history to be lost forever.

I Never Heard Any of Them Say That They Regret What They Did

Spirit Trickey-Rowan, a well known citizen from Little Rock, was interviewed by me on Wednesday, November 29, 2006. I interviewed her by phone. I happened to pick this particular person because she is the daughter or Minnijean Brown Trickey, one of the Little Rock Nine. Spirit also has so much knowledge of the Little Rock Crisis in 1957 because she works at the museum. I trust and know Spirit will have good details to tell me about the Civil Rights Movement and that is why I chose her for my interview.

Interviewer:
Sarah Martin

Interviewee:
Spirit Trickey-Rowan

Time Period:
1950s

Location:
Little Rock, AR

Affected Group:
African American

Setting:
School

To begin the conversation, I greeted Spirit and began to ask her questions. I asked her what she knew of the incident of the Little Rock Central Nine Crisis in 1957. Spirit pretty much gave me an overall summary for the story with some quotes and feelings her mother, Minnijean, felt during the incident. She began with telling me about the year of 1954. In 1954, school segregation was the law, until the *Brown v. Board of Education* Supreme Court Case. They changed this because it had a negative impact on black students and they noticed the problems with segregated schools. Teachers needed more pay and African American students needed an education.

Three years later, the plan to desegregate came into action in Little Rock. The year before that, in 1956, Hall and Horace Mann were built. Hall was built for white students and Horace Mann was built for the blacks. But they still wanted to desegregate because, for one, Central was the most beautiful high school and it had more students graduating and going to college. As Spirit said, "They wanted to know what they were missing."

Minnijean, the mother of Spirit, actually came from Horace Mann. She wanted to go to Central because it was in walking distance of her home, she had friends who wished to go there, and she was seeking for a better education.

Spirit continued with the detailed story of the crisis of 1957. The plan actually started off with several dozen African American students. Then, the court brought it down to 17 because of the bad grades and bad conduct of the students. Then, it was brought down to only nine because the court limited their extra-curricular activities and parents were being threatened of losing their jobs. All the kids were thinking was, "Hopefully they will accept us."

Governor Faubus then called in the National Guard to stand outside of Central High. Then, a young lawyer by the name of Thurgood Marshall paired up with Daisy Bates to remove the guard. On September 23, 1957, the police had control of the day at Central. They actually took the nine students through the back of the school and into their classrooms. But the teachers wanted them out because it caused too much chaos, so the police drove their cop car into the school with a mob right there on the vehicle the whole time. Spirit quoted her mother by saying, "It was one of the most terrifying moments of my life." Then, on the 25th of September, President Eisenhower sent the 101st Airborne under federal order to stand outside the school and walk the black students around the campus.

School went on and Minnijean was suspended in December for dropping chili on boys at lunch because they would not let her pass for they had their legs in the way. She then came back, and in February, she left the school. A group of white girls followed her to the third floor and one picked up her purse and hit Minnijean in the head. Minnijean then called them "white trash." She finished her high school years in New York. The students were treated cruelly by a majority of the white students, but some were nice also.

The next question I asked Spirit was her opinion of the whole problem. "Stupid," she said. Spirit has heard the nine students talk several times and she said, "Personally, as sad as it was, I never heard any of them say that they regret what they did." For Spirit, and me as well, it enabled us to go to school with other races today and choose the school we wish to attend. It also shows "There has been progress." Ironically enough, Spirit works now where her mother was turned down of her rights and education.

The last and major question of our interview is what she thinks should be done to stop all civil rights problems in our lives today. Spirit told me that a few weeks ago she was interviewing Jesse Jackson. She asked him the same question as I asked her for she also wished to know. Jesse told her, "Work on your character." Spirit agreed and understood what he meant. She says, "Character means something. Treat others the way you want to be treated." Also she believes to get an education. Because we are able to, we should take advantage of that. The Little Rock Nine made it possible for us to go there as one and get an education to further our future.

Even though Spirit may be young and did not suffer through the crisis, she still is knowledgeable about it all. She is trying to carry on what her mother stands for equal rights for all people. Spirit works as a Park Ranger at the Central High National Historic Site, allowing her to keep up the family tradition. All she is trying to do is educate people on the incident and tell her mother's side of the story. Along with her husband, Travis Rowan (a.k.a. Tre Day) they try to spread the words of equality for all people and give back to our community.

How Far We Have Come

It was a Thursday night after a game, when I called my grandmother, Rose Booth, to interview her about the civil rights issue. I got straight to the point by asking her about her childhood and her school. My grandmother did use a few words that stuck out to me. She used words like "overcrowded," "pre-primer," "segregated," and the phrase "more opportunities."

Interviewer:	Daisha Booth
Interviewee:	Rose Booth
Time Period:	1950s
Location:	Little Rock, AR
Affected Group:	African American
Setting:	School

My grandmother grew up in a rural area. It was segregated, and only black people lived there. The school that she attended was not the best school for anyone. There were students from the elementary level to the high school level all in one building. Their books were never new because the school couldn't afford them, so they used the white schools' old books. There were no major athletics either. All that they had was basketball and softball.

Her story of going to a K-12 school and being raised the way she was is connected to the larger picture of the integration of Little Rock Central High. During the Lost Year when all Little Rock schools were closed, the black students that went to Horace Mann had to transfer to her school, Nelson High School, which caused major overcrowding.

Since it was over the phone, I couldn't see her face during the interview, but, in her voice, there wasn't any change in her tone. If there were any emotions that she felt, it would be relief that she could grow from living in a segregated world to where she is now. I think that her purpose in sharing the information that she had was to show how much has changed in her lifetime. She went from growing up in a countryside area and attending a segregated school to living in the city and being able to have options and to think for herself. She wanted to show that even though she was probably mistreated by whites, she learned to "treat all men equal and to know that all men are equal."

When I asked my grandmother how the civil rights movement as a whole helped her grow as a person, she said that it has presented a lot of opportunities for her as an African American to do things as simple as going places that she couldn't have gone when she was younger. She was glad to see that her children had more options than she did. My grandmother had first-hand experience of living in a segregated world. She lived to see the day that her children and grandchildren have a lot more opportunities than she did, and she is proud of how far we have come.

Central is Probably Better Now

When I walked down the steps and saw my mom relaxing on the couch, I knew it was going to be a very laid-back interview. It was evident that my mother was prepared for the interview by way she glared at the television. I explained the Memory Project to my mother and she agreed to do it.

Interviewer:	Jessica Lovelace
Interviewee:	Karen Lovelace
Time Period:	1980s
Location:	Little Rock, AR
Affected Group:	African American
Setting:	School

As I explained to my mom what the interview was about, her back was rested on the arm of the couch. Occasionally she would turn from the TV and look at me as I was talking. My mom was wearing her Race for the Cure t-shirt and her comfy, black pants with her hair pulled back. She looked very comfortable and easygoing. This made the interview easier for me.

My mother is a Central High School alum. She graduated from Central High in 1981. I thought it would be a good idea to ask my mother what Central was like when she went there. I felt it would make a good interview. In my opinion, it did.

"Central is probably better now, but when I was at Central things were still segregated. Things were better than the 50s and the 60s, but things weren't as good as things are now," my mom explained. Then she told me what things were like when she was at Central. She said that a lot of events were separate, like dances, picnics, and other events. The white and black students didn't really interact with each other. The Student Council members tried to make things more diverse. But because of the way things were at the time, people didn't try to change. "It wasn't right, but we just didn't want to ruffle anyone's feathers," she said. "A lot of black students didn't join a lot of clubs because they didn't feel welcome," she added. I was really shocked when I heard this.

My mom told me a story about one of the plays they had at Central when she was there. It was called "South Pacific." The parts for the black student were limited to slaves and servants. Many of the black students in Drama didn't get to participate in the play, which made a lot of people very upset. This story stayed in my mind because I thought that Central was more diverse in those days. Considering the way things are now, this story was very surprising to me. I'm glad things have changed since then.

Central has come a long way since 1957. Everything isn't perfect, but things are certainly getting better. That's why it is important to remember the past, so that we don't repeat it in the future. Hopefully, I will have an interview with my children explaining to them about change and how things are getting better in our society.

Pieces of the Puzzle

My great-grandfather was already walking into the small room assisted by a petite African American woman when I slowly took my seat on his couch. He was extremely healthy for his age at 90 years old as he confidently made his way across the room to his favorite and most comfortable reclining chair. Carefully placing himself in the chair and pulling back the recliner lever, he looked over to the woman standing in the doorway. "I'll come back later to take you down the hall to eat, okay?" she said. "That will be fine...thanks," he softly replied.

As he moved himself into a comfortable laid-back position, I could see that he was wearing his hitched up pants and the ever-so-familiar plaid shirt, worn out from all the years it has gone through. It made me think how worn out my grandfather must be from all the years that have gone by in his long life and the memories that he has picked up along the way. A small table stood by the chair with an unfinished puzzle waiting for his next move. His white hair was almost shining in the dim light provided by the lamp, casting shadows across his face. "Well, are you ready?" he said enthusiastically. My great-grandfather was ready to take me back in time to a whole different world, all in the private and comfortable setting of a nursing home in the place where it all began...Little Rock, Arkansas.

Ford Nelson was born in 1914 in a small town called Nakona, deep down in Texas. As he grew older he got a job working in an auto body shop where he spent many years working to pay his way through school and to help his family out with financial aids. Later on in his life, he ended up getting married to a woman named Mamie. They had one daughter, Cloreesa, and they all lived happily in Nakona.

As much as he knew about what was going on in Little Rock with the integration, Ford did not experience much of it himself. Ford

Interviewer: Michelle McCain

Interviewee: Ford Nelson

Time Period: 1950s

Location: Little Rock, AR

Affected Group: African American

Setting: School

happened to grow up in a town where no blacks were in sight. All of Nakona, Texas, was resided by whites. In fact, he barely ever saw any blacks at all. However, he still heard many stories of what was going on in Little Rock over the phone with his sister (who lived in Fayetteville then) and in the back of the old auto body shop. The small town was intrigued with the news. Gossip about the happenings spread like fire through the streets. "There was small talk everywhere," he said, "...over coffee and on the breaks during work." He squinted his eyes as he thought back.

"As the years went by, Cloreesa got married and they stayed with Mamie and me in Nakona." I could already tell just by his tone of voice that my great-grandfather was beginning to sift through a strong and meaningful memory far back in his life. He said that even though it may not seem very significant, it was a very clear and memorable moment for him. Cloreesa had just told him that they were moving to Little Rock. Ford paused, and then slowly went on. "It was too dangerous at that time...I was not a happy fellow, of course. Back then I wasn't too fond of blacks either." To him, at that time, all the blacks were doing were causing danger and trouble. Even today he says, "I don't know what all the fuss was about." In other words, he believed that the whole thing was blown out of proportion.

Ford may not have known it then, but this small moment would affect his life greatly. His attitude had even slightly changed toward the blacks. He was never against African Americans because he had never met one, but by what he was hearing, it was not good. Now that his daughter had moved into the danger and violence, he got more protective and kept up with the news back in Little Rock. "I could remember hearing the news about when the National Guard was called in. Everyone thought that the government should not be getting involved," my great-grandfather paused and looked up to the ceiling. "And I agreed." He said that later on he would move to Little Rock, too...after it was all over.

Near the end of the interview, the African American woman came back into the room. "Are you ready, Mr. Nelson?" she said. "Yes, I've built up quite an appetite." "Alright, I'll be right back."

As she left the room, my great-grandfather looked to me. "Now, in my life, and America itself, things are different. Blacks and whites get along these days. They help each other with jobs or simple things like crossing the street...and help an old man like me get to the cafeteria dining room." He gave out a small laugh as he climbed out of the chair.

As I sit back on the soft, tan couch and listen to my great-grand-father talk with the woman in the door, I begin to think of all the years to come. I realized that maybe not everyone always experiences or knows a lot about what is going on in the world. However, no matter what it is, it will always affect you, whether you are right there in the middle of it, or out on the borderline, just listening to the conversations in the back of an auto body shop. We can always pull through any struggles in civil rights, just like getting through the era of the Little Rock Nine. America just has to put their mind to it, and all stick together as one nation.

Listen to your elders, your mentors, parents, librarians, teachers, neighbors, even the man that works at that coffee shop across the street. Everyone has a story to tell...it is your job to listen and hear the effects it has made on them, on yourself, or on the United States itself. Life is like the puzzle sitting on the small table next to that favorite chair of yours; and memories are like the puzzle pieces. At the end of each day you get a new puzzle piece...and you can't finish the puzzle until have all the pieces. Your life is not whole without those significant puzzle pieces filling in the spaces.

The Story of the Women's Emergency Committee

M rs. Margaret Kolb is 78 years old. She was born on November 27, 1927. Mrs. Kolb lives in a big white house at 224 Colonial Court, across the street from Travis Gray and me. Mrs. Kolb was a stay at home mom around the time Central closed and civil rights was occurring. That is what Mrs. Kolb told Travis Gray and me.

Interviewer: Kristen Smith
Interviewee: Margaret Kolb
Time Period: 1950s
Location: Little Rock, AR
Affected Group: African American
Setting: School

In the year after the Little Rock Nine left Central, Governor Faubus passed several anti-integration measures, including one that would allow a vote of the people to close any school. So Central was closed. The Little Rock School Board resigned in frustration over the closed high schools. Some mothers of white students were frustrated that their children were not in school. These mothers were also frustrated that black students weren't allowed in the school either. Soon Adolphine Terry founded WEC, The Women's Emergency Committee. The first WEC meetings consisted of twenty or so mothers. The WEC office was at 224 Colonial Court, in Margaret Kolb's garage. The WEC only had a mimeograph machine, two typewriters, a desk, and a telephone at night. The women worked all day, everyday.

They were forced to do things in secrecy or behind the scenes because of the fear that the White Citizens Council would find things out. The WCC would watch the women from behind the telephone poles and followed them home. The WCC would also watch the garage from the streets, and tapped the telephone lines.

During the Lost Year, the teachers signed a contract to go back to work every day, so they had to sit in their classrooms during school hours even if kids were not there. While this was going on the WCC set up private schools in old nursing homes for the white students, and Central still had practice for the football team every day.

In late 1957, teachers were fired from Central for doing one thing: they all agreed to teach nine black students during the year before.

The men in Presbyterian Church started STOP for the forty four teachers left at school. STOP means Stop This Outrageous Purge.

The WEC and STOP worked together. Later, when the schools were reopened, Margaret Kolb started an integrated PTA, even though people tried to destroy it. Mrs. Margaret Kolb also opened the first integrated swimming pool in her backyard.

Because of everything Mrs. Kolb had done, her children were harassed at school. One time her daughter got in trouble for "fraternizing" or playing with black kids. Margaret Kolb's husband, Dr. Payton Kolb, was also affected by this situation.

Mrs. Kolb meant a lot to me before the interview. She was the little sweet old lady who would make apple pies and bring them to her neighbors who just adore her. Now she means a whole lot more. Hearing her story about the challenges she and everyone faced around her and about everything she has done in her life for Central High and blacks is just astonishing. The story has changed me some; I have more respect for Mrs. Kolb and everything that has happened at Central.

Because of the Racism, I was Frightened to Go to America

My interview with my father, John Doe, took place on March 22, 2005. My father was lying down on his bed, and I was sitting on a chair with all the windows open in the room. The air conditioning kicked in when I was about to ask a question about the integration so I decided to wait until the room was cool. As it got cooler and I got ready to ask questions, my father took a sip of water that was on a stand next to the bed and he told me to go ahead and start.

Interviewer: John Doe
Interviewee: John Doe's Son
Time Period: 1950s
Location: Vietnam
Affected Group: Americans
Setting: News

My father, who was in Vietnam during the integration in America, had learned about the integration in Vietnam with his classmates. He started telling the story of how he learned about the integration in 1957 in Vietnam, and then he said, "I was 12 years old at the time of the Central High integration and the teacher always keep the class up to date on what had been happening in America. She would tell us about racism and how they are also against Asians and not only African Americans."

"The Vietnamese newspaper," he said, "was made up of news from America and some current news of Vietnam." He told me that he had felt sorry for the African Americans who had to suffer through the integration and all the racism, and then he told me, "Because of the racism, I was frightened to go to the United States during the early '70s, but I wasn't scared to go to Europe or even Canada."

I can tell that my father had gone through times where he had encountered racism because he would stare up to the ceiling and not look up at me, and he would become quiet for a while. He then got up to refill his water and that was when I told my father that I was done.

When he was about to leave, he told me, "I know how the African Americans felt during segregation and how the Caucasians were racist." I could see now that his choice to go to the United States when racism was still bad was a difficult choice for my father, and it took courage for him to stand up to people who are racist. Now I can also see how my dad felt during his move to the United States and how he could connect to how the African Americans felt when they were treated poorly.

Chapter Two:
Beyond Central

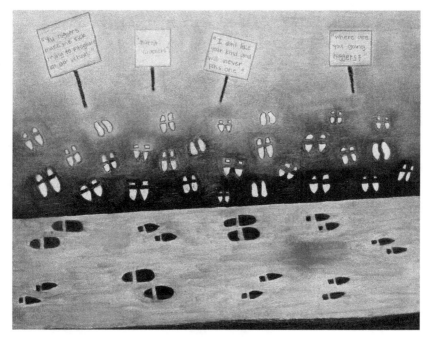

In Their Footsteps
Rae Plugge

Editors' Commentary

L ittle Rock Central High might have been the most publicized example of conflict over segregation in schools, but it was not the only place where tensions were high. Before *Brown v. Board* was passed unanimously by the Supreme Court in 1954, only 16 states prohibited racial segregation and 17 states required it. The transition from a separated society to an integrated one proved to be extremely challenging. Schools were the first battleground in a conflict that never really ended. Today, the students and administrators from the schools carry experiences almost identical to, but not as well known as, those of Little Rock Central High. Protestors fought integration and new private schools were made just for white children. The children who were part of the first wave of integrating schools encountered many of the same challenges that the Little Rock Nine had to. This chapter deals with the students who overcame daunting obstacles and a system set against them, and the teachers who dealt with the change. These essays, more broadly, deal with an extensive societal change, spearheaded by children who courageously pioneered acceptance and fought for equal rights.

Ala'a Abu-Rmaileh's essay tells the story of O. C. Duffy, who dealt with discrimination at the University of Arkansas at Fayetteville. His essay is instructive of the hardships that those who integrated schools first had to go through for an education, and how racism permeated Southern life. The white students had no real motivation for their cruelty besides conditioning, and in Duffy's experience, it can't be overcome. Freddie Fulton's essay shows the struggles that the black children who were integrating schools went through. His mother was tormented for being an intelligent black girl by the white kids and the black kids, showing the boundaries of racial solidarity and the racism endemic to the education system. Amanda Abernathy's essay goes into some of the same territory as Freddie Fulton's. The essay deals with the difference between desegregation and integration: how black students and white students went to the same school, but kept as far apart as possible. Even after segregation officially ended, white parents didn't want their children to play with black children, and white children still taunted black children. It is also from the perspective of an outsider without preconceived prejudices and exemplifies the fact that racism is learned. Krystal Clark's essay about Claudette Simmons shows the change that failed to happen in Amanda Abernathy's essay. After the students had a difficult year, the students became more accepting of the small group of black students, and they assimilated, dressing and acting like the white students. This experience mirrors the immigrant experience; in a way, after a period of discrimination, they're accepted and are able to assimilate, gradually giving up their unique ethnic identity. Perla Vargas had to deal with an institution that was desegregated, but not integrated. She was admitted to Johns Hopkins University, but was kept out of student life by chilliness from the mostly white student body. Her story about discrimination at the University of Arizona shows that any foreigner, even a student at the graduate level, was discriminated against by educational institutions.

Racism permeated the education system and negatively influenced the grades of many capable black students in integrated schools. Jay Withers' essay shows how Donnie Jean Murray received a poor grade on an assignment because she was black. She was able to rise above the teacher, challenge her grade, and force the teacher to give her the grade she deserved. Sandy Becker, in Glen Becker's essay, was not allowed to take the National Merit Exam because he was black, even though he had outscored the next candidate (a white student) by several points. In these essays, it is the parents and school administrators who clearly harm the futures of African American children. It goes back to the issues discussed in Anna Keogh's interview. Her essays points out that there are great consequences from desegregating schools without integrating the community—that is, without breaking down barriers of mistrust, resentment, and fear. In these communities, especially in the absence of leadership by adults, both black and white students suffered. However, the black students usually suffered more. Jasmine Price's essay deals with a woman who had to struggle a great deal in school. Her buses would leave without her if she didn't show up at the right time. She pointed out how oppressive the society was to blacks then and how the burden for work is higher now for blacks than it is for whites, and that the society we live in still has significant strides to make to make up for past wrongs. Vanessa Bastidas' essay focuses on how the topic of race relations was nearly unacceptable in schools during that time. When a teacher brought the subject up, the class immediately became tense, and the tension was instructive to Sharon Mayes about how issues like race can affect relationships and be damaging. Her fear of hurting people's feelings contributed to the tension.

Central—Unified
Andrew Hamby

Closer to Normal: First Impressions of Cultural Acceptance in the United States

I had just finished working on an assignment for my Civics teacher when he told me that he would prefer that I interview my mother, Perla Amalia Vargas, a Mexican born immigrant. He wanted me to ask about any instances in which she had been mistreated because of her race or origin. I was glad to comply; learning about one's past through simple listening is much more interesting and fun than cutting out dozens of articles from a newspaper and writing paragraphs on them, the way I was having to make up my work. When my mother and I sat down, I decided to put my note taking aside. It would be much easier, I decided, to merely pay attention to her while she spoke, therefore not making her slow down or lose her train of thought.

Interviewer:
David Robles

Interviewee:
Perla Amalia
Vargas

Time Period:
1980s

Location:
Arizona

Affected Group:
African
American

Setting:
College

We talked for a while, but she told me over and over how no particular story stood out in her mind. She told me how she was "pretty much always outcasted," as she put it. "When I was at Johns Hopkins University," she said, "I was the only Hispanic I ever came in contact with. When I would say hello to people in the hallway, no one would respond. In a similar way, I noticed that the African American custodians would never look at or speak to anyone else in the halls and no one would acknowledge them at all, either."

Upon my asking how she handled this, she told me, "I stayed persistent. I said hello to everyone, regardless of whether they responded or not. I looked everyone directly in the eyes until the administrators finally gave in and began treating me closer to normal. As for the cleaning people, it took the woman who took out the trash in my office almost a year to finally respond to my 'thank yous and 'hellos.'"

Among these stories that my mother told, one really stuck out in my mind. When she was in college at the University of Arizona, my mother was a teaching assistant who graded papers. At the time, nearly all the teaching assistants at the university were foreigners who spoke English as a second language. Many of the students at the school were complaining about their grades and claiming they were not graded fairly or correctly. Although there was no problem with the immigrant student teachers who graded papers, the administration at the school decided it was politically easier to blame these people than to actually argue against a problem. Because of this, my mother and the rest of the teaching assistants had to go to an English culture seminar and take a test.

"It was degrading and insulting. They treated us like we were stupid and we let them know we didn't appreciate it," she said.

Although she easily passed the test, my mother still resents the school board using the "outsiders" as scapegoats.

After hearing her narrative, I realize that however small, racial mistreatment is always remembered. My mother, Perla Vargas, experienced just that; and small or not, she bravely rose against it.

There Seemed to be Quiet Tension

We were in Mrs. Mayes' house on a fall afternoon. She had her windows opened so there was a slight breeze in the house. I was sitting across from her in her living room. Right before our interview, she had begun to cook dinner so there was still a tasty smell in the air. Mrs. Mayes sat down beside me and looked interested in what I had to say. We both just listened to the birds outside until I began my questioning.

> *Interviewer:*
> Vanessa Bastidas
>
> *Interviewee:*
> Sharon Mayes
>
> *Time Period:*
> 1960s
>
> *Location:*
> California
>
> *Affected Group:*
> Caucasian
>
> *Setting:*
> School

Mrs. Mayes grew up living in California, but was born in Massachusetts. In the late 1960s, she moved back to Little Rock, Arkansas and has been living here for about 40 years. She has four kids and a large number of grandchildren. She grew up going to school with blacks, whites, Hispanics, and Orientals, so she was used to integration. When she moved back she noticed the difference in the community and in the attitude of the people about integration. Mrs. Mayes is in her fifties and she is a gardener for people's houses. She is a very kind lady who likes to help people out a lot. This is her story.

The purpose of this interview was to learn and record Mrs. Mayes's experiences in the fight for civil rights. Her experiences are a part of history and I was there to record it. We talked about a variety of subjects including interracial dating, prejudiced people who changed, school, and many other topics. These topics were, at times, personal, but contributed a lot of information to the interview. Mrs. Mayes's experiences have made up an important part of history.

Mrs. Mayes remembered many interesting events that had happened to her over the past 40 years. She recalls when she was in high school her entire class had to participate in debates over an array of subjects. One day, the instructor brought up the topic of integration and segregation. Her class was full of different races and they might have thought about the subject before, but not for discussion. The teacher wanted to know everyone's opinion and so she began by stating a question. Mrs. Mayes remembers feeling nervous because she didn't want anything said inside the room to affect the relationships with her friends in the room. Mrs. Mayes said that the blacks in the school actually didn't mind segregation. She said to me that it was probably because they had never experienced it; then their views would have probably changed. This also described Mrs. Mayes quote, "There seemed to be quiet tension," because Mrs. Mayes noticed that a lot of topics that could have been brought up were avoided, probably so no riots would start. Mrs. Mayes' experience was just one of the many that had affected her life.

This experience changed Mrs. Mayes' outlook on life. She learned about other people's perspectives and so now she likes to know about the opinions of other people. Mrs. Mayes has always been a person to think about people and always likes to help them. This experience has let her know the other side of the story. Before, her attitude toward everyone was "not interested," but now she knows that this was a bigger part of her history that she needed to know. Now her attitude is to acknowledge everyone's opinion.

The history of America's struggle for "liberty and justice for all" was created by the individual stories of people like Mrs. Mayes. You might not think that a debate in class can relate to this bigger story, but you're wrong. This little classroom situation showed exactly how the nation was behaving during that time period. Everyone had their own opinions about a topic and they would fight for it. The only difference was that the fighting that took place in the classroom was verbal and was used to prove a point wrong. In other words, the debate was just the smaller version of America struggling for "liberty and justice for all."

This interview has increased my knowledge of the points of view of different people during the struggle for "justice for all." I used to think that what happened in the past really didn't matter to me because it was in the past, but that's just like me saying that what I do now won't affect me in the future. This interview definitely changed the way I think, because now I am more interested to learn about more stories that people have over the fight for civil rights so I will like history more.

The Unforgettable Past

The person I interviewed was O. C. Duffy. He's an African American at the age of 61. His occupation is a professor in mathematics at Pine Bluff University. His relationship to me is that he is a friend of my mother's friend.

After I introduced myself to him, I started asking him some questions about his life during the Civil Rights Movement, and his response was as follows: "I was in school during the Central High situation. I was 14 years old and I remembered National Guard trucks passing by. I was chopping cotton and I wasn't at school at the time because it was summer. I lived in West Memphis, between Memphis and Little Rock. I didn't know what was going on

Interviewer:
Ala'a Abu-Rmaileh

Interviewee:
O. C. Duffy

Time Period:
1960s

Location:
Fayetteville, AR

Affected Group:
African American

Setting:
School

at the time, but the next day, news about the Central High integration made national news."

He continued, "Nothing happened to my family, we were living in a rural area, and there were no integration in the schools at the time. There were many problems for a long period of time. Central High rejected black students. There was cautiousness on both sides, because no one knows what things may happen. After the incident, everyone was afraid. We didn't know what to do, but there was a sense that God would protect us." I asked why integration happened. He responded by saying, "It was obvious that black schools were second to white schools. Black schools would get used books, and a lower level of education than the white schools got. So they thought integrating the blacks into the schools, the level of education would improve."

He continued, "I remembered a lot of personal things that affected my life. I graduated in 1965, and I used to work for a company in Arkansas. I remember I went with two white gentlemen to eat lunch, they went into a restaurant, ate their lunch, and brought mine and I had to eat mine at the steps, because I was black and I wasn't allowed.

At the age of 13, I was chopping cotton with my mother in a farm owned by white people. The lady brought some water, it was a very hot day; she gave water the dogs first, and then offered us some water. My mother refused to drink and told her we don't drink after dogs. I was the first black to graduate as a civil engineer from UA Fayetteville. There were many events that happened there. There was a song ["Dixie"] that blacks thought was racist. President Nixon was visiting UA Fayetteville and some of the black students refused to get up from their chairs to allow the band to get in and this started a riot in the university. I was the first black in the civil engineer department; a white student invited me to see a play and insisted on me going there. The play was about four white students, but one of them was dressed as a gorilla. The teacher will give them a test and the white students will get 98 to 99 percent, but the gorilla will get 20 to 30 percent. It took me a while to understand what was going on. The gorilla represented me. The teachers at Fayetteville took care of the issue professionally. Otherwise, if the other black students found out about this, it would have started a riot. I graduated from high school and went into the University of Pine Bluff mostly for black students to study mathematics. They selected two black students to study at UA Fayetteville. I didn't want to go there, because I hated UA Fayetteville. I remembered sitting with the teachers. They were telling me that I would never graduate. But I insisted that I will graduate even if I have to take an hour/semester. It took me eight years to graduate as a civil engineer."

He continued, "I looked at the scenes from when I was a child. It's kind of confusing, from a religious point of view; if we are all Christians, how can we hate each other? As I got older, I realized that people used Christianity to cover so many things. The racial situation has changed some but it has a long way to go. Racism is still engraved in the old generation. I don't know about the young generation. Money controls everything and white people control the money and unless we have money to do things we'll always be second hand citizens and we'll never be independent."

He concluded, "It gave me a sense of reality at a younger age. The world isn't fair and people are unfair in this world. I was asked one time while I had a job in California, and I was the only black person there, what's the solution to the race problem? My response was: it's engraved in the older generation. All of this made me grow faster and stronger. If you want to succeed, you have to make an individual sacrifice. I work now in Pine Bluff University, though it's less money and farther away from my home but I do it, because the black students need me more than the whites."

I learned what it was like over 50 years ago. The story means to me how sad it was it was for him to grow up in such harsh conditions just because he was black, and it made me change the way I think today. Also, it made me see how we can be unfair to each other.

Suspended

It was a bright, spring morning when Alice Marie Fulton and I met in the living room with the TV off and everyone else out of sight. We sat across from one another, but soon she was called out (the toast was burning). I remember telling my mother of this project and that I needed her. She gladly accepted and set a date. After being called out, a 50 year old woman who is loved by most came through the open door.

She walked through and got comfortable on the couch. I then asked her where she lived during the Civil Rights Era. She said, "I really just lived in Little Rock, Arkansas, until my family moved to Hot Springs."

Interviewer:
Freddie Fulton

Interviewee:
Alice Marie
Fulton

Time Period:
1950s

Location:
Little Rock, AR

Affected Group:
African
American

Setting:
School

The next question was "Where did you feel the most discrimination?" "Mostly here in Little Rock," she said, "but it was nothing I couldn't handle." I then asked when she felt like when she was being picked on. "When I started middle school," she said, "since I was a little smart, I was put into classes with most of the white kids. That is what started most of the kids at my school picking on me."

She sharply said, "They used to call me 'Smart Alice,' white and black, and also 'burnt cracker.'" I asked her how she made it through the years she spent at that school she glanced at me with a burning look and quietly blurted, "My mother's strength. One day though," she told me, "my mother wasn't there and soon after I got to the bus stop I heard whispers and repeatedly got hit by hard, cold rocks. So after I could not take any more I took my biggest book," she said softly, "and threw it at the closest person I could then I dropped my bag and threw my fist at everyone I could."

The wrong thing about this story is that within the next week, word got out and Ms. Fulton was suspended from the school, but the worst news was that the kids that were throwing rocks could still go to school. They were not even suspended for a day.

"After this incident, my mother didn't even let me finish my suspension before she took me out of the school altogether. I did not let this bother me though. I packed my new books and went to school the next day, but the thing about it is that word must have gotten out to more than just my school because from that day on, no one tried to pick on me."

The last question I asked her was "How do you think this has changed you as a person and if you had to do it all again, would you change anything?" "I believe this experience has made me a stronger person and now I really try not to let people mess with me as much as I did. The only thing I would have changed about this experience would be to not let as much rocks hit me as I did," she said laughing, "because I think I still have a bruise from this incident."

I Was Afraid This Had Ruined My High School Education

Patrick J. Keogh, my dad, sat in the comfort of his home as he retold his high school experience in a rural southern town. Patrick Keogh grew up in Marianna, Arkansas, near West Helena. In the early 1970s, Lee Senior High School integrated. Most of the Caucasian families did not support the integration, so they built a private school, Lee Academy. Lee Academy was priced so that not very many African Americans could afford to attend. Patrick Keogh was one of 150 Caucasian students to stay in the 1,200-student high school.

> *Interviewer:*
> Anna Keogh
>
> *Interviewee:*
> Joseph Keogh
>
> *Time Period:*
> 1970s
>
> *Location:*
> Marianna, AR
>
> *Affected Group:*
> African American
>
> *Setting:*
> School

When my dad was in 10th grade at Lee Senior High School, there was a walkout. African American school officials wanting more jobs open to the black race caused a three to four month walkout. Many students of Lee Senior High School were prompted and prodded to help with the walkout and many did. "90% of the school walked out," said Patrick with scorn.

"I remember that I was in Algebra and all of the sudden a bunch of black guys were running [through] the portable buildings. We were all scared because they had turned the fire hoses on them, knocking people down. They were even throwing trash cans at them," Patrick Keogh said sadly as he told about the first day of the walkout. From then on there were only 10% of the students left, and nothing to do all day.

"All I did was play chess and basketball, but my Algebra teacher did give homework every night," Patrick Keogh said bitterly. My dad was extremely bitter toward the walkout; he did not understand why he still had to go to school when everyone else didn't. Eventually, most of the students and teachers came back. The African American school officials did not get what they wanted, but some students like

Rodney Slater (Clinton's Secretary of Transportation) never came back to Lee Senior High.

Some people say that high school was the best time of their lives, but for Patrick Keogh, it was a nightmare. He said that he has tried to put Marianna, Arkansas, behind him. The minute he could, he wanted to get out of the town and never come back. He has returned to Marianna, Arkansas, in recent years, but was instantly embittered and saddened when he saw Lee Senior High School again. Even through all of the things that happened to my dad, he still is the most kind and wise person that I have ever met. I respect him to the fullest; and even though I don't know exactly what he went through, I could see and feel the tension of bringing up that place that he had long ago stopped calling home.

My dad said, "I was afraid that this had ruined my high school education."

I Remember Those Times... But It Could've Been Much Worse

For this assignment I chose to interview my Aunt Jean because she grew up in the South where most of the racism and prejudice occurred. When I visited my aunt in Newport, Arkansas, I thought it would be a good idea to get her point of view of how she felt about what was happening at the time. She is currently a teacher at Newport High School.

My aunt's first experience of racism was when she was about six years old. In Pine Bluff, where my aunt grew up, most public places had two bathrooms: one that said "Colored" and one that said "White." The water fountain for whites was clean and the water fountain for coloreds was filthy, and was clearly not equal to the other one. Even though the "separate but equal" law was in effect, not everyone went by it. She also remembers when she would travel out of town. There would be signs for whites only at restaurants, or African Americans would have to go to the back to get served. Often, blacks would not eat at the restaurant because they would not give in to being treated unequally. I remember my aunt saying "If they won't serve us like everyone else, I'm spending my money elsewhere."

When I interviewed my aunt about the Civil Rights Movement, she said she was a young girl at the time. "When I was in school, I didn't have to go through as much of the discrimination because I lived in a dominantly black community, but there was some racism. In 1968 at Merrill High School, white teachers started working for the school and would come and interact with the black students. No white students attended. In 1970, the schools were forced to completely integrate." That's when she saw more and more white students at the school she attended.

Interviewer: Jay Withers
Interviewee: Donnie Jean Murray
Time Period: 1960s-1970s
Location: Newport, AR
Affected Group: African American
Setting: School

A lot of times, the teachers would already predetermine what grade the African American students would get. "Once a week, we had to write a theme for my reading/writing class. Mine was entered in the Pepsi-Cola contest and I won first place. The next year I asked my new teacher if I could use the same one that won me first place and she said yes. When I turned it in to her, she said it was too bad to grade. I was crying for the rest of the day. I then went to an African American teacher and asked her to grade it. She gave me an A- on it, so I took it back to Mrs. Roberts and showed her the mistake she made, and against her will, she had to give me the grade I deserved." This displays the prejudice there was against black students back in the time. The white teacher unfairly said that the paper my aunt wrote wasn't gradable, but when she took it to another teacher she found out that Mrs. Roberts wouldn't grade it simply because she was a black student.

The same teacher taught my dad at the University of Arkansas at Pine Bluff. She treated her black students similarly to the way she treated my aunt. Rather than look over the individual student's work, she would just give all them B's on their work, regardless of whether it deserved an A or a lower grade.

Back in those days, there would always be some sort of mentor to encourage the black students to be the best they could be. "My mentor would tell us, 'We have to be better than our white counter-parts, otherwise you wouldn't even have a chance.'" Black students were influenced by their mentors to study harder, make do with the situation they were in and excel in all they do. Most importantly, not to cause any conflict between whites.

From the stories my Aunt Jean has told me, I have learned that I am very fortunate to live in the time and place I do now. Back then, black people were not treated the same as whites. There were lynchings and beatings that went on that I do not have to live through. A lot of people have suffered through the segregation, racism, and dis-crimination throughout the years simply because a certain group of people did not like the race of African Americans. Today, however, racism and prejudice are not as big of an issue as they were back in the '50s and '60s when my aunt was growing up. It was drastically different from how we are being brought up. My views on segregation and racism have changed some. Now I realize more how difficult it was to black students in a predominately white school. I've learned to see that life was much harder in those times and that we should treat one another with respect and dignity.

Black People Were the Lowest Life on the Planet

After deciding to interview my granny, I had to call her over the phone since she stays in my home state, Missouri, and I live in Arkansas. Alice Henry grew up in Bell City, Missouri, but as a child, she lived in Indianapolis for a short while. When Alice was a young adult, she encountered first-hand the labor of picking cotton and working in a field, but was paid for her labor. This mother of six knew what it was like to grow up in a time where people of her race weren't respected. Currently residing in Sikeston, Missouri, Alice has worked at Hunter Acres Nursing Home for many years. Now she is content with being a nanny for toddlers and taking care of her mother (my great grandma), Mama Dear.

Interviewer:
Amanda Abernathy

Interviewee:
Alice Henry

Time Period:
1960s

Location:
Missouri

Affected Group:
African American

Setting:
School

Many times, my granny had to pause a while before answering questions or topics during our interview. This could be because she had to think hard to remember, or because these experiences brought back so much emotion. My granny's experiences with segregation and racism took place in the early 1960s when she was about fifteen years old, my age. When I asked her, "What kind of changes did you see happening where you lived?" she responded, "I had a lot of white friends when I was a young girl from living downtown before living on a farm. While Mama worked for the Huff's [a white family who paid her mother 'Mama Dear' to clean and cook] I would play with the young white girls that were my age, but their parents didn't want them to play with me." Her school was integrated, but it could have easily been segregated because the whites and blacks did not interact or talk. At first, the blacks couldn't even play sports with whites but after a long wait, the school district integrated sports.

One story in particular that really stuck with me was her story about an older African American girl at her school. This girl was always bullied by a Caucasian male and he never thought that the girl would do anything back when he bothered her. One day, this boy called the girl a racial slur and the bullied girl had enough; she hit him and he fell down the stairs. As my granny says, "She gave him a sucker punch and he never forgot it." After a few laughs, I asked my granny, "How did you feel at the time all of these things were happening?" After a moment of silence my granny said sympathetically, "I felt different from the other kids…I was from Indiana and there it was always integrated. Nobody paid attention to color and said 'you black' and 'you white' so I wasn't as exposed to prejudice." She also stated that "the farther south you went, the worse things were." With this said, she believed that Arkansas was probably worse than Missouri.

After reminiscing, my granny started telling me about how she feels about everything now since she is mature enough to look back on what has happened. She stated, "I thank God for people like Martin Luther King Jr. … I really do." I also asked if these experiences changed the choices or her perspective of situations now that she is older. She replied, "Yes, it taught us to respect other minorities. Black people were the lowest life on the planet. Then the Indians, now Mexicans and Latinos; All of this taught me that God made us equal and in order to gain respect someone has to give it."

My perspective of history and even my granny was changed by this interview. I learned about the things my granny had to go through to earn the respect she has now. I never would have thought that a loving, funny, and always smiling person like her could experience something so harsh and still turn out to be a great person who respects all races. People today are still struggling for their respected civil rights and I believe it's up to me and everyone else to keep others' best interest in mind and learn to respect everyone as individuals, not as a certain color or ethnicity.

Scipio A. Jones to North Little Rock High

In the late 1960s, there was a wonderful woman who goes by that name of Claudette Simmons that was a part of the integration that was going on. She had to experience a lot of the hardcore integration that went on in the '60s. I interviewed Ms. Simmons over the phone and I interviewed her because I was very interested in her past experience. Ms. Simmons is an unmarried woman with four grown sons and daughters and has eight grandchildren. She also has had very good jobs. She had worked as a National Guard for 24 years and she worked at the V.A. Hospital for 22 years in North Little Rock. She worked as a patient assistant in recording data. Ms. Simmons helps poor kids and also goes to Bible class. Ms. Simmons is also going to school to become an addiction therapist to help young people. But when she was younger she also went through some rough times.

Interviewer:
Krystal Clark

Interviewee:
Claudette Simmons

Time Period:
1960s

Location:
North Little Rock, AR

Affected Group:
African American

Setting:
School

When Ms. Simmons was about 15 years old, she was living off Hickory Street in North Little Rock, catching the city bus to an all black school named Scipio A. Jones High School. Scipio A. Jones only held grades 7-12 but she and some of her other schoolmates had to be switched over to an all white school named North Little Rock High School which held grades 10-12. She was already switched over when she came back from her Christmas break. She had to go from Scipio A. Jones High to North Little Rock High School.

In 1968, she was transferred to this all white school full of angry white kids. The white kids booed them because the "freedom of choice" was what sent them over there. The blacks had to go to the school because they couldn't graduate from Scipio High. The white kids spat on the blacks and walked on different sides on the hallway, away form the blacks so they wouldn't have to touch them. After a while the white kids were afraid to call the black kids niggers so they called them the "boogy bears" and as they said it, they held their hands up as if they were frightened. So, Ms. Simmons and other black kids used to meet up over at Daisy Bates' house to talk about the situation and to find a way to stop it. But, they just kept going to school. Ms. Simmons was angry because they were cheating them. She thought that everyone should be treated the same, no matter the color of their skin.

After a year passed, the whites finally accepted the black students for who they were. As the white kids started to change, so did the other black students. The black girls started doing what the white girls did. The black girls started carrying purses and dressing like the white girls. The girls were also able to get on the pep club (drill team). The black boys also dressed like the white boys too.

To this day, Ms. Simmons barely thinks about her past experience. But there were two events that happened to her dealing with her jobs. When Ms. Simmons was on her job, there were white people that worked with her that acted like they were better than her and that made her think back to 1968 when the whites used to act like that. But this event happening kind of built up her confidence. The second big event that happened dealt with giving a job to a white person. Ms. Simmons was training in this building with my Auntie Lisa at one point when Ms. Simmons had to train a white girl for a promotion. When they tried out they gave the job to the white girl because she was white. Then Ms. Simmons filed an EEO because that wasn't fair. But Ms. Simmons found out that she had the highest ranking over 25 others and the girl she trained was in second. But that event reminded her of her past.

I learned a couple of things from this project. I never knew that all this was happening in North Little Rock and I didn't know that the white kids were afraid to call the black kids niggers and they called them the "boogy bears." The person I interviewed, Ms. Simmons, went through a lot in the past and it's good to see her still standing strong to this day trying to help us young adults. The interview didn't really change as we were talking but she didn't mind telling me of her past. So to this day, Ms. Simmons will never forget her past and the NAACP (Nation Association for the Advancement of Colored People).

Other People Were Blocked

Sandy Becker is a nice, caring man. He is a hard worker and believes in himself. I interviewed Sandy (who happens to be my dad) at our house, Wednesday, November 30, 2006. I picked Sandy Becker to interview because he seemed to know a lot about civil rights. As Sandy was growing up, he experienced civil rights. Sandy Becker is an international auditor and a CPA for the Little Rock School District.

Interviewer:
Glen Becker

Interviewee:
Sandy Becker

Time Period:
1970s

Location:
Camden, AR

Affected Group:
African American

Setting:
School

Sandy Becker was born in 1960. At the age of five, Sandy lived in Camden, Arkansas, in the middle of the Civil Rights Movement. He remembers when Dr. King, Jr., was killed and remembers being told when President Kennedy was assassinated. Sandy Becker in 1970 attended an all black school in Stephens, Arkansas. Also in 1970, Stephens' black school was integrated with another white school in Stephens. And so the black school became the elementary school for blacks and whites and the high school, which was 7th-12th, became the high school for blacks and whites. Sandy also mentioned that prior to this, black people stayed to themselves and white people stayed to themselves.

There is one particular story that Sandy Becker wanted to share with me. In 1979, Sandy Becker graduated from high school in Stephens, Arkansas. Many students in his class took an ACT test (one of the college tests they took). There were several with high points Sandy told me. And in fact, Sandy Becker wound up being salutatorian of his class. However, only one person was permitted to take the National Merit Exam. And that particular person was white, Sandy pointed out. He outscored this person by at least three points on the ACT test. And yet that was the only person allowed.

"Other people were blocked," Sandy said, but he had tested high enough to where he felt that he should have been able to take the National Merit Exam. However, he was passed over because they only wanted to promote one person from the school. At that particular time, the person could not be black. And that was something Sandy Becker looked at and he said to himself, "Things are not always equal." And it galled him that the National Merit Exam was something he was never allowed to test for and he was not allowed the opportunity to compete nationally for scholarships. And it had to do, Sandy told me, with peoples' preferences and prejudices.

Doing this Memory Project helped me learn more about how civil rights affects every one. This project allowed me to get closer to Sandy Becker and to see how civil rights affected his life. My civil rights view changed a little bit toward the subject because I never knew that civil rights affected someone so close to me.

Struggle and Heartache

The time is 6:13 p.m. on a cool, sunny Sunday evening. The room is tranquil, with the only sound being the cars whizzing by the open window. The only people in the room are just my beautiful grandmother and me. She sits there, gazing out the window, pondering whatever questions I would ask her. She looks somewhat calm and serene with the gray streaks in her hair glistening in the sunlight.

My grandmother grew up in the small, country town of Hollygrove, Arkansas. She is the middle child of ten children. Growing up in a little shack in the middle of town, she was a well respected young lady and was pretty popular in high school. She did not enter college, but decided to attend numerous vocational schools which contributed to her being an airline consultant for Southwest Airlines today. She has been working there for a little over a decade and enjoys her job of helping customers get the best deals on plane tickets. I was surprised that she even had the time to do an interview with such a busy work schedule as hers. The purpose of this interview is to give yet another side of the story as it pertains to the Civil Rights Movement. The topics discussed were home life, public places, and the educational system of Hollygrove, Arkansas, and how that compares to today's society.

After the interview, there was one portion that really stuck in my mind. I noticed that my grandmother talked a lot about her adolescent life. She always compared how she lived to how I live now. "You young people these days don't know nothin' 'bout struggle and heartache. These days ya'll can just press a button and the whole world is in your hands, literally. Back then, you had to work for what you had and that is the exact reason why things are the way they are." That statement made me think about what all we had in this 21st century. I asked her how old she was and where she was when civil rights

Interviewer:
Jasmine Price

Interviewee:
Patricia Price

Time Period:
1960s

Location:
Holly Grove, AR

Affected Group:
African American

Setting:
School

started happening. She said, "When the unfair part of civil rights (where Blacks were being treated unfairly) was when I was attending grade school, our school was so far away from home and my brothers and sisters, and I walked back and forth from school to home every day. We eventually started riding the bus, but our buses weren't as nice as the ones you have now. If we missed the bus, it was either a butt whooping or a walk. Therefore, I never missed the bus. Back then we worked hard at school, so we appreciated it more."

When asked about the changes in civil rights, she started getting a little aggressive. "Back then, everything used to be separate. We had separate drinking fountains, separate movie theaters; we even had to walk on the street if a white person was walking on the sidewalk. At the beginning of the change, nothing much was different, but gradually, blacks were given more opportunities to do something with their lives. I remember it wasn't the things that people said about black people, but it was they way they looked at us." When she said that comment, I thought, "The way people look at others now is not that much different. Now, people are so judgmental of others. So that hasn't changed." When asked how she felt, her reply was, "At the time, I was young so I did not really understand, but as I started getting older, I was frustrated at times. It was so hard for the black community to come up. Now as I am older, I feel like blacks have as equal of an opportunity to be successful. We just have to work a little harder to keep what we earn to get..."

This interview changed my way of thinking as it pertains to history and the struggle of civil rights. When I talked to elderly people, they sometimes told of stories that they been through back in the day. For some reason, I never really appreciated the values that I have in today's time period until I had this interview with my grandmother. Now I know how I need to better appreciate the free education that I am receiving. I do not have to walk to school, receive outdated, beat up school books, and I can be challenged. By having this interview, I am now more aware and can better appreciate the values of 21st century living. My advice to anybody doing an interview is to listen. We have two ears and one mouth for a reason. If you listen with your two ears, then your one mouth can pass down history into someone else's two ears as well.

Chapter Three:
Beyond Schools

The Irony of the American Flag
Jessica Boyd

Editors' Commentary

This category centers on the broad legal enforcement of segregation within the United States. Jim Crow was an ubiquitous legal concept that applied to nearly every aspect of life in the South, from separating things like hospitals to separating how people walked down the street or greeted each other. The fact is that most stories about discrimination that we could collect with this project take place outside of school and in the neighborhood or at the store or in the workplace, and this very noticeable division merited creation of a section of its own.

Bobby Dunn's essay enumerates some of the most common offenses against African Americans during the Civil Rights Movement. Dr. John Forrest Henry Jr. pointed out that, as disgusting as it was, even hospitals were segregated during that time period. Paul McCormack described the variety of opinions held by the general public about African Americans. Even Nancy Rorex, who was close to a few African Americans admits that she was "an unconscious bigot" because she just went along with the ideologies that were presented to her since birth. Many times, the idea that racism is inherent at birth has been used to justify racism. However, there are many instances where that fact has been proven to be blatantly false. Just in this chapter, there are six essays which prove that racist ideas were instilled by parents or older community members when children played with or dared to love members from another sex. In Max Farrell's essay, the town his mother was from destroyed her relationship and caused her to move back to Arkansas because they found out about her black boyfriend. Pure acceptance, like the kind found in Amanda McClendon's essay with the little girl who described her friends by the colors of their shirts rather than the colors of their faces, should have been universally lauded, but in many instances, it was squashed. Additional essays which exhibit initial acceptance with reprimand from higher authorities include those from Lindsey McIntosh, Neelam Vyas, Briana Williams, and Adam Thannisch.

A recurring reason for racism seems to be that the racists thought the minority they were rejecting was of lesser value. They were scared that the alleged cheapness of the minority would rub off on them and their actions support this conclusion. In Alexandra Gordon's interview, one day her Big Momma has had enough of the lack of respect given to her and she fights fire with fire in protest of her mistreatment. Ann Sullivan's interview makes it clear that the Massachusetts public has rejected the newcomers for several centuries: first the Irish, now the Portuguese. This lack of acceptance isn't just present in Massachusetts, though, as shown by Jennifer Thompson's interview with Carlos A. Lopez, where he recounts his nightmare in New Mexico when he was turned away from a store because he looked Mexican. The new immigrants were often considered stupid and unfit to be Americans. In the military, it was a bit easier to gain respect as a minority because the job of a soldier is so demanding that the men tend to work together despite obstacles that would have kept them separated at home. Meaghan Karney, Jim Curry, Brenna Gilstrap, and Livingston Anderson all discuss the ways that the different branches of the military managed to incorporate all races. Although a few nasty comments were exchanged at times between races, nothing escalated to the extremes at home or abroad.

The use of religion to justify slavery [by Southerners before the Civil War] has associated the white Southern clergy with racism in the minds of many, and their pleas for "moderation" during the Birmingham Bus Boycott only furthered that perception. However, Alex Boyd's essay shows activism by the white clergy, who were attempting to move their parishioners and the public toward tolerance, and it also shows how small gestures can open eyes. His essay was included in "Beyond Schools" due to the primary action being the turning away of a black family and the conflict between the white churchgoers and the preacher, rather than the focus being on activism. The preacher's gesture of acceptance toward the black family, however, is worth a great deal of attention. Small steps like what the preacher took can end up making the most powerful changes in lives, as the essay shows. Mackie O'Hara's essay has several things in common with Alex Boyd's. It goes into how small steps can create larger changes. The story about the newlywed couple who left their reception to be with the black best man because Lincoln and Joset Munro left is very touching. Their small steps show that it takes the action of a few to convince others to also take action, and how important it is to take those small steps. This important theme gets further attention in the final chapter of the book, as well.

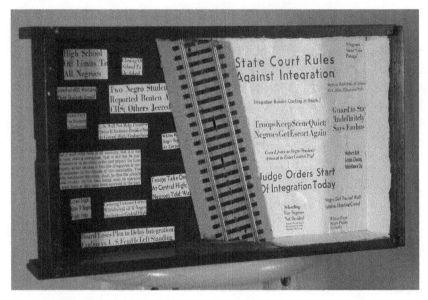

Opposite Sides of the Track
Gabriel Goldman

At a Point in Time, I Felt Bad About Being Black

In 1950, Herma Jean Cannon was born in Little Rock, Arkansas, to a poor mother and father. They lived in a one bedroom house and had no electricity. Ms. Cannon's mother worked for a white family as a maid and received very little pay. Her dad was a worker on a farm and he too made very little money. As Ms. Cannon grew old enough to attend school, she attended a small school with about ten kids. "Times were very hard, and textbooks were hard to come by," states Ms. Cannon.

Interviewer: Lindsey McIntosh
Interviewee: Herma Jean Cannon-Martin
Time Period: 1950s
Location: Little Rock, AR
Affected Group: African American
Setting: Store

During the 1950s many changes occurred around Ms. Cannon. "Whites were acting superior to us. About this time my family became very protective of me. They did not let me do as much as my friends did. I stayed in the house so much," Ms. Cannon sat back in her chair and a day dreamy look crossed her face. I became puzzled. Why was she looking like this? Was she happy about the things she went through in her childhood?

Finally, I got the courage to ask about the look on her face. She replied, "About this time is when I met a young white boy. He was so handsome."

"Really?" I asked in an interested voice.

"Sure. It didn't last though, honey. That boy's daddy found out. I remember when that boy's father spit on my daddy just because he found out that we were black. We were walking to the grocery store and the man just spat on him and called us the N word. That memory stayed with me for a long time and it always will."

After Ms. Cannon told me this the whole little incident just kept racing through my head. I felt so bad for her. I then asked Ms. Cannon to elaborate on her story. All she said was, "At that very moment I felt like dirt. I cried all the way home. All I could think about was my dad and that man arguing. I still feel bad about that day now. At a point in time, I felt bad about being black."

Civil Rights in Black and White

He's intelligent, thoughtful, and serious. He's honest and sincere. He's interesting and unique. He's Finis Eugene Fultz, my great-grandfather. Eugene, as everyone calls him, was born December 2, 1925, making him almost 81 years old. Although he has had several different jobs, he spent most of his life as a butcher. As a young man growing up in his home state of Oklahoma, Eugene witnessed integration in America first-hand. I chose to interview my great-grandfather because I knew that he would have many experiences to share with me, and he would be open to express his opinions. I interviewed him while he was in town this Thanksgiving at my grandmother's house.

Interviewer: Neelam Vyas
Interviewee: Finis Eugene Fultz
Time Period: 1930s
Location: Oklahoma
Affected Group: Caucasian
Setting: Neighborhood

My great-grandfather has had many experiences, many stories to tell, but few have heard about his life during the civil rights movement. Few know of his views, his values, his feelings during this period. That soon changed, however, when I talked face-to-face with this witness of time.

Born around a time when race riots were common, my great-grandfather heard many stories about conflict between African Americans and Caucasians. He said that whites were very defensive against blacks. He even knows of an exact spot in Oklahoma on Cincinnati Street where black men were held up against a wall and shot to death. The white citizens would tear up the black section of the city.

With his dad making only a dollar a day, my great-grandfather was born into a pretty poor family. He grew up as a minority in a black neighborhood. He said that in the 1930's he had personally integrated during this time. His best friend was a black boy across the street called Lil' Jessie who he played with all of the time. He associated with all people regardless of color.

Even as a teenager, my great-grandfather remembered signs that read "Whites Only" or "Colored Only," and how African Americans were forced to sit in the back of restaurants. Unlike many white people at the time, however, my great-grandfather had African American friends. He said that he went and sat with black kids just as much as he sat with white. He also said that there was always a lot of fighting and shooting in his neighborhood, but he remembered that whenever his dad would have to leave town, his black neighbors would always promise to watch over his mom and siblings.

By the time my great-grandfather was grown and had his own house (in an all-white neighborhood), the real integration began. The black neighborhood was six blocks from his new house, but there was a movement into the white settlements. When this occurred he was told that his property, which was originally worth $30,000, had fallen drastically in value to $15,000. During this period, my great-grandfather remembered neighbors saying things such as "I don't want them niggers living next to me" or "My property isn't worth a dime now." In addition to the large change in property value, my great-grandfather also faced other financial problems. After 26 years of service from his insurance agency, they cancelled his home insurance. Their only reason was that there were problems around there. He and his family chose to physically move their house to a different neighborhood to increase its value and so that they would be able to receive affordable insurance.

Since he had always lived near colored people, my great-grandfather didn't really see any changes happening in his surroundings. This probably explains why he didn't have trouble integrating. He didn't actually know segregation or prejudice. He never remembers a fuss between whites and blacks growing up because there were no whites in his neighborhood besides his family. He grew up in a family that taught that everyone is equal, and we are all God's children made in his image and likeness. He also tried to instill these same morals in his children.

My great-grandfather still sees discrimination today. In fact, one of his own sons used to love hanging out with African Americans as a young boy, but has made a 180-degree turn and can barely tolerate them now for whatever reason. My great-grandfather says that we just need to leave other people alone and let them live how they want to live. "There isn't someone I don't like," he said. "There's good in everyone."

Through conducting this interview I have learned a lot about my great-grandfather. I didn't know that he grew up in a black neighborhood for one thing. I was supposed to learn his views on the subject, but I didn't quite know what to expect. I'd never asked him about his life during this time, since the topic of segregation is almost considered taboo in modern society, but I have changed my views about my great-grandfather. He has really inspired me to do what I think is right and that I don't have to follow the crowd. I now see him in a new light because I didn't realize how open-minded he is. He has also given me a lot more to think about in the subject of civil rights. He said that there are still problems dealing with civil liberties and discrimination today, and it's up to our generation to take charge and fix them. "It isn't my worry anymore; my era's over," he said.

Painful Friendship

Arbie Moore is an LPN, mother, and my grandma who has gone through many times in her life that involve civil rights being violated. She is a wonderful woman who is at the ripe age of 53. She informed me that the event she was describing occurred in 1961 or 1962. At the time she was a resident of Morrilton, Arkansas, and Morrilton was (and still is) mainly a town of white people. At that time, Morrilton was a town that had no problem with discriminating against a person because of their race. The big problem was that my grandma was black.

Interviewer: Briana Williams
Interviewee: Arbie Moore
Time Period: 1960s
Location: Morrilton, AR
Affected Group: African American
Setting: Neighborhood

When Arbie was about seven or eight years old, she was living in Morrilton. Every day, she walked to and from the school. She walked alone because she was the only one in her family at that time that attended school. She had many brothers and sisters, but because she was one of the oldest, she had to defend herself. One day, when she was walking, she saw a boy walking behind her. She was not the first one to speak in situations like this one so she just continued to walk. As she walked, all of a sudden, she heard the boy shout, "Hi, my name is Andy, what's yours?" And they instantly became friends. For many days after that, they walked to and from school talking. Andy's dad had heard from one of his neighbors that his son was spending most of his time with a black girl. Andy's dad did not allow his family to talk to anyone outside their race. Therefore, the next day he watched his son walk to school with the black girl and then he took all his anger out on his son. He told him that he should not hang around [racial slur], and if he did it again he would not live to see tomorrow. The next day, Arbie hugged Andy and he shrieked because he was in pain. His dad had beaten him. Andy told Arbie everything that his dad had told him, but told her he still wanted to be friends with her. My grandmother told him that she wanted to be friends with him, too, but not if it was a life or death situation. Andy was the best friend she had, but she did not want him to lose his life over her. She told him she would miss him with all of her heart, but they could not be friends.

When my grandmother told me this story it made me realize that she was not just an LPN, mother, and grandmother. She is a caring person. She did not go through the problem her friend did, but she did put his safety over her heart. Andy was truly the best friend she had at that time and it is hard to lose a best friend at all, let alone willingly. I never knew what my grandmother had gone through, but I will learn more about what she had to go through. I now know why she is an LPN; she cares so much about people that she wanted to take care of the sick. I admired my grandma before, but now she is my role model.

I Was in Love, Despite the Racial Barrier

M y mother was alive during the Civil Rights Movement, but she was just a young child. I interviewed her at our house in central Little Rock. We sat on my gray couch with the video camera placed in front of us. It was a sunny day so the sun was shining brightly through the windows. My mom was very open about her past, not showing much emotion on some things that were life changing. Somehow, she found most of the events to be humorous.

Interviewer:
Max Farrell

Interviewee:
Olivia Farrell

Time Period:
1970s

Location:
Paragould, AR

Affected Group:
African American

Setting:
Neighborhood

Olivia Farrell was born and raised in Paragould, Arkansas. She was never really aware of the outside world or of the changes in civil-rights occurring all across the United States. Her parents raised her not to discriminate in many ways. When black entertainers came into town, her parents would host them rather than the white ones. They also never said negative things about other races, unlike most Paragould parents. The nondiscrimination hurt my mother in the long run. When she went off to college in the early 1970's, she went to Maryville College in Maryville, Tennessee. It was a very diverse liberal arts college. That is where her troubles started.

Olivia had no problems fitting in at Maryville. She gladly accepted all races. She even had a black boyfriend. That is where her troubles came from. "I was in love with Michael, from Georgia, despite the racial barrier." My mother was calm when she talked about the subject because she knew that it was over with and that things turned out all right the way they are now. Olivia told her parents about her new boyfriend, and the townspeople of Paragould found out. They were angry that there was a racial mixture between a citizen and another race. The citizens of Paragould took to action. People began a boycott of her brother-in-law's clothing store and her father was at risk of losing his job with the Army National Guard. Even the Paragould Chamber of Commerce was threatening her father. Her parents told her she needed to "end the relationship immediately." Her parents refused to pay for tuition for Maryville College and said she had to go to an in-state school.

Olivia's rebellion kicked in at that point and she desperately fought to stay at Maryville by asking for financial aid. She even thought of staying and getting a job in Maryville, rather than going to school, just to stay with Michael. My mother's emotions still maintained relatively calm as we spoke about these life changing events because she knew things turned out well as is.

Her intellect overpowered her rebellious mind, and she decided to transfer to Hendrix College in Conway, Arkansas. Olivia stayed in close contact with Michael. They frequently talked over the phone. One night she called him and said, "Let's get married." He said, "No," and that was the end of their close relationship. Olivia still tried to maintain a friendly relationship with him, but over time they grew apart and faded away from each other. She wound up meeting other men and Michael did the same with women.

Since they don't communicate anymore, my mother doesn't know too much about Michael. She briefly mentioned that he was married. Now my mother is divorced with two children and is quite happy.

After listening to a part of my mother's life that I really hadn't heard before, I wondered about some things. I wondered if she would still be with Michael if the citizens of Paragould didn't bother her or her family about it. I also wondered what would have become of me if that did happen. I skipped over that thought quickly because I didn't want to think about it. Now things are really good for everybody in my family, except for the divorce. Everyone overcame the obstacles to succeed in life. I suppose it is a happy ending after all, but I still wonder about the "what ifs"...

From being involved with this Memory Project, I learned a lot about people and that everyone has a story to tell. I realized that one disagreement or argument can change an entire life. After hearing my mother tell of her struggle, I thought about how things are today. Everything that was unequal or wrong in the 1950s-1970s has changed. I learned that I should treat older adults with more respect because I don't know what they have gone through. Most adults have experienced a traumatic moment in their life that could still be a painful memory. Treating people with respect earns more respect. It is something I have learned while completing this project and I will hold it in my mind.

The First Time I Saw Her

There I sat on the couch, April 16, talking to Ann Sullivan, learning about her experiences with Civil Rights. I sat there in my pajamas, listening to quite calming music, thinking about what my Grammy Sullivan would be doing. I imagined her running around the kitchen cooking and cleaning anything she possibly could. I also pictured my Grammy Sullivan's curly gray hair with her little round glasses on her face. I pictured her wearing one of her cute little floral dresses with tiny Keds shoes. Finally, we got to talking about civil rights and everything that she experienced related to them.

Interviewer:
Keely Sullivan

Interviewee:
Ann Sullivan

Time Period:
1950s

Location:
Massachusetts

Affected Group:
Irish, African, and Brazilian Americans

Setting:
Neighborhood

My Grammy Sullivan first told me about Ireland because she lived there for the first years of her life. "Ireland was completely different from America; the people, community, and natural surroundings," she said. She described the vast, hilly environment back in Ireland and the busy, hectic life in Massachusetts. "In Ireland there really were no black people," said Ann Sullivan. She then told me about her uncle's experience with racism. "In the early 1920s my uncle came to the United States from Ireland. When he started looking for jobs in Boston, written on the windows of stores was 'No Irish Need Apply,'" she said. I then learned that earlier in time Irish immigrants were treated just as many Hispanics are today. There was not only racism to African Americans but also many other ethnic groups years ago.

Ann Sullivan, now living in Framingham, Massachusetts, told me a little about her life and her experiences with racism and civil rights. "I came to America when I was 17 years old in 1949, I really didn't see very much racism back then," she said. She then told me about some of the elders living around her. My Grammy Sullivan, speaking in a soft voice, said that many elders think of African Americans as being different from Caucasians. "I think elders think that way because they are not exposed to very many African Americans," said Ann Sullivan. She then told me, "African Americans are human beings. Just because they are black does not mean Caucasians are better than they are." I was not surprised at all by my Grammy Sullivan's remark because she is the type of person who treats anyone and everyone the same regardless of their race or ethnic background. I learned many things about my grandmother's different experiences with racism earlier in her lifetime.

Ann Sullivan then told me about her life currently in Framingham, Massachusetts. "Recently, more African Americans and Brazilians have moved to Massachusetts," she said. She explained to me that when she first moved to Massachusetts there were not many African Americans, but now there are more and more African Americans living in Boston, Massachusetts. "Now I always hear stories about people not renting out apartments to African Americans just because of their race," said Ann Sullivan. The tone of my Grammy's voice was soft and it sounded like she was ashamed to admit the racism that is currently going on around her. She then told me about Brazilians currently living in Massachusetts. "Brazilians work hard to earn their money, then they send it back home," she said. When saying this, my Grammy Sullivan told me that all the Brazilians living by her are very hard workers and that they are in Massachusetts to make money, not to cause any problems.

The interview I had with my Grammy Sullivan over the telephone was really informative and interesting. It amazed me how there was still racism going on around her. I had not realized that there are less African Americans living in Framingham than there are African Americans living in Little Rock. It shocked me hearing that Irish immigrants used to be treated so terribly and that African Americans were still being treated differently. Today, I wish that everyone would look at each other the same, because I know there is still a lot of racism around the world. We are all people and should be treated the same. Doing this interview project taught me a lot about racism in my community and the communities around me.

I Didn't Understand Why

"The changes occurring in the time frame of my childhood and even into teen years did not impact me unfavorably. I was not the one being discriminated against. Instinctively, I knew that there was something 'different' between me and the black kids because I was brought up to think that there was a difference. But, I didn't understand why, except for color and that I couldn't play in the streets with them or have them as friends. They would walk through my neighborhood, look longingly at all the toys, bikes, wagons, etc., that I had, and I suppose they were wishing they could have the same. Maybe I felt some sadness for them but I didn't know how to show it because we kids were not allowed to engage them as friends or someone to play with.

Interviewer:
Bobby Dunn

Interviewee:
Jim Broadus

Time Period:
1950s-1960s

Location:
South Carolina

Affected Group:
African American

Setting:
Public

"I can only speculate that the same mental attitudes were impacting my cousins, friends, and others in the same situation. We were brought up to maintain that separation due to color.

"I can still picture in my mind the instances of riding on the street cars and busses. The blacks were required to ride in the rear. In my years of 12, 13, and maybe 14, my sister and I were permitted to go to the movies (then known as 'picture shows') on Saturday afternoons. We would walk up to the little area know as Crichton, catch a bus to go to the theater, know as the Roxy. The blacks would always sit in the rear. It was just accepted and there were no disturbances, questions, or unwillingness on their part. They just did it. At the time, it did not affect me all that much. In later years, as I have looked back on it, I have tried to put myself in their position and have concluded that it must have been hard on them, the adults maybe, but the black kids didn't know any better.

"As best I remember, it seems the issue of blacks voting would come up in family discussions. And, they were not given the same privileges to vote. At such a young age, I could not understand why they could not.

"At the time all of this was happening, I didn't think too much about it. All of us were brought up in such an environment of separateness that it was a second nature. They lived in their neighborhoods and we lived in ours.

"One thing I did think about and that was the blacks that my parents had doing chores. My mother had a black lady come to do ironing and housework. She was also charged with taking care of me when she came home from work in the cotton mill. I can just see her now: a nice lady who seemed to like what she was doing for us. And there were black men who did work for my dad and grandfather, cleaning yards, ditches, and heavy-duty stuff. I know my parents paid them, sometimes in money and some times in goods like vegetables, meat, and milk, because we grew or raised all of these things.

"Also, I once heard one of my grandfathers who lived in Mississippi talking about the blacks he had working for him. They were really hard workers who helped him 'peddle' meat in his horse and wagons, and collect sap from pine trees that went into making paint and things like that. While they were not classified as 'slaves,' it was clear to me that the blacks would do anything my grandfather asked. They were, in a word, dependent of him for a living.

"As I've grown older, I have thought a great deal about the events in that time period. As I grew, entered segregated grade school, high school, and college, I could sense, especially in high school and college, that something was happening and that change was going to occur. In 1957, I graduated from Spring Hill College, it was integrated. There were not too many blacks initially, but the numbers grew in later years. Spring Hill was integrated after the University of Alabama.

"Shortly after I graduated from college, I was drafted into the Army. This was to be the most significant exposure to integration that I had ever experienced. I was shipped off to Fort Jackson in South Carolina. In my company of about 200 men, there were all races including whites, blacks, and Hispanics and we were all truly integrated. In my tent of about 15 there were blacks and whites. We slept in the same quarters, ate together, trained together and everything else someone does in a military environment. I actually made friends with some of the blacks. They wanted the change as much as we did. And, to the best of my memory, there was never a fight or unruly behavior because of race.

"As a commander of a Field Artillery Battalion in Vietnam, some of my best leaders were blacks. I recalled one specific instance, and there were others, where I relieved a white sergeant and placed a black in charge.

"All of this pluse the experiences I mentioned earlier has changed me forever. From being brought up in a very segregated environment, not one of hatred, but one of racial differences, to an integrated military career, I knew that if I wanted to succeed there could be no discrimination, real or potential. I still go back to the first days of my basic training at Fort Jackson, through the ensuing nearly 25 years, working with and associating with the black community was to be a way of life. There was to be no turning back the clock into the world of discrimination."

Wondering Why

Paul W. McCormack is 59 years old. He is my father. He currently lives in Little Rock, Arkansas, where he owns his own business. He was born on April 11, 1946. He grew up during the Civil Rights Movement and attended a segregated school. He experienced much of the hatred that was present in our country during that period. He had an amazing story of what he went through as a young man living in America at that time. This is how my dad's story was related to me.

My father was a military brat. He moved a lot during his early years. He lived in Japan, Washington, California, and he eventually settled with his family in Hope, Arkansas. In 1960, he was a ninth grader at Hope High School. His high school was a segregated school. The black children in Hope attended Henry C. Yeager High School. Henry C. Yeager High School was not necessarily a bad school, but my dad remembers feeling bad for the black children who attended this school because he knew their situation was inferior to his own.

In the town of Hope, whites and blacks had separate everything. It was not limited to the school system. They had separate bathrooms, water fountains, entrances to public facilities, and even separate Bibles to swear on in the courthouse. My father remembers one store proprietor in Hope who loved to tell him about how much he hated black people. He would explain what white people should do to keep black people in their place. My father was told that black men should step off the curb into the street when a white man walked down the sidewalk. The store owner thought black people should be hung from a telephone pole if they got out of line. It was plain to see the extent of hatred there was that white people felt toward black people.

Interviewer:
Madison
McCormack

Interviewee:
Paul W.
McCormack

Time Period:
1960s

Location:
Hope, AR

Affected Group:
African American

Setting:
Neighborhood

My father particularly remembers the movie theater in Hope. Black people and white people were seated separately in the theater. Black patrons had to enter through the alley way and sit in the balcony. He also remembers the restaurants. He said that on one occasion two black boys attempted to enter a restaurant. One of the local white hoodlums beat them and threw them into the street. My father really couldn't believe how these people were being treated. He wished he did not have to watch it go on but felt powerless to do anything about the situation. He hoped for change.

There were more horrible acts which my father would witness as a young man in Hope. All of my father's relatives were southern whites and the vast majority of them thought along the lines of what we have come to know as "southern white thought." He remembers thinking at times that his relatives were supportive and compassionate toward black people, and there were other times when they were hostile and not so kind to black people. He remembers his uncle being very good to his black sharecropper and his family, but he is not certain how good his uncle would have been if his sharecropper had not done what he told him to do. There were times when my father witnessed his own cousins chasing black children from Fair Park, the city park at Hope. The treatment of black people was horrible. There is no other way to say it.

The incidents of white power and domination over black people passed over a period of about 20 years as schools and businesses slowly but surely integrated. The Civil Rights Act signed by Lyndon B. Johnson paved the way to give black people an equal footing in the South. It was slow in coming but thank goodness it came to pass.

My father graduated from Hope High School in 1964. It's hard to believe, but the school was still all white at that time. *Brown v. Board of Education* was the Supreme Court decision handed in 1954 which declared that separate but equal schools like those in Hope, Arkansas, would not stand as they were not equal. The crisis at Central High School occurred in 1957; however, integration was to be a very slow process. My father's younger brothers graduated ten years later; Hope High School was finally integrated at that time.

When I was interviewing my father, I realized that what happened was really a crime. I am very happy that it is not like that anymore. I do not know what I would have done if I had to watch that happening to someone who was just trying to live a happy and enjoyable life like everyone else. The white people took that opportunity away from black people. They were always trying to keep black people down and in "their" place. I wish I could have been around to try to stop what was happening or maybe I would have felt helpless just as my father felt helpless as a young man in Hope, Arkansas.

In conclusion, the interview with my father has shown me how civil rights in America are an issue for everyone, including my own family. My father in his lifetime lived through the evolution of civil rights that has resulted in the many freedoms that minorities enjoy now. I have learned a great lesson by studying the way it was in comparison to the way it is today. We have come a long way in creating freedom and equality for all Americans, not just a few. However, we must never forget the past and should vow that such events will never happen again.

Hate of Faith

The interview took place in my busy kitchen. I could hear the washer and dryer noisily going. Our old and clunky dishwasher was loudly washing dishes and our air conditioner was blowing furiously. We were sitting at our hard wood kitchen table in wooden chairs. We were sitting beside the window, and it was about midday so the sun was brightly shining through the shades. You could also hear the birds chirping outside. Our windows were open so you could smell the cool fresh outside air. It was a beautiful day.

Interviewer:	Alex Boyd
Interviewee:	Michael Boyd
Time Period:	1960s
Location:	Pine Bluff, AR
Affected Group:	African American
Setting:	Church

There weren't that many people in the room with me. It was just me, my dad and my mom. My dad was the one I was interviewing and my mom was busily making our lunch.

My dad is short and broad-shouldered, with a wide chest. He loved to play basketball and was very athletic. His athleticism still shows; he has large arms, wide shoulders, and a very big chest. He has little hair and is cleanly shaven. He smiles often but can unintentionally have a very serious look on his face. He likes to have fun but takes a lot of things seriously. He also loves to dress nicely. He had just come home from work when the interview started. He was wearing a button down shirt, a sports coat, a tie, black pants, and nice shoes.

Michael Boyd is currently in his early 50s. He lives in Little Rock, Arkansas, on Saint Charles Boulevard. He is presently an accountant at the State Highway Department. He graduated high school and earned his Masters and Bachelors Degree. He was born January 1, 1957. Michael Boyd was born and raised in Pine Bluff, Arkansas. Michael's dad abandoned him and his mom before his third birthday and his stepfather had a terrible alcohol problem. His mother, Carma Boyd, had to raise him and his stepbrothers on her own. Michael attended Pine Bluff High School and graduated to go to Hendrix College.

My father talked about the racial issues that were occurring around him during his childhood. Going to Pine Bluff High, of course, there were many issues that took place. Many of which he was included in, but not in a bad way.

One thing that sticks out in my mind is that members of my father's church turned a black family away when they tried to enter the doors. The next Sunday, the preacher stated that they were all God's children, and allowed the family to enter.

The year was 1967; my dad was ten years old. It occurred at a small southern Methodist church in Pine Bluff. It was a normal day, with my dad, grandmother, and all his step brothers attending church. Little did they know that an unfortunate incident was about to occur.

The trouble started when an African American family tried to enter the church one morning. The entire congregation (excluding my dad and his family) blocked the door and would not let them in. "They called them awful names, names that made my older brothers shudder, and brought tears to my mom's eyes," said my father.

The reaction from the pastor was not exactly what the congregation had expected. My dad said that "the next Sunday, instead of going along with the planned sermon, the pastor made up his own sermon concerning the past events. He said that we are all children of God and as long as he is pastor, everyone, whether they are black, white, blue, or green, is allowed in the church and that if we are turning away our brothers and sisters in Christ, we might as well be turning away Christ himself."

The experience really opened up my father's eyes. He was fairly young when this occurred, so his mind was still developing and unsure of many things. This experience gave him a strong foundation for making the right decisions in the future. Today Michael Boyd is a respectable, successful man that sees things from all points of view and is not quick to judge. His attitude is fair toward others, no matter what color. This experience helped change Michael in a good way.

The story stuck in my mind because it made the most sense to me out of all the other stories he told me. I share the same beliefs and faith as my dad, so when he told me about someone being turned away from a church by its congregation, it shocked me enough to stay with me. And the speech that the pastor gave the congregation made absolute perfect sense to me. The congregation was no better than the people they turned away and humiliated. If they are doing that to them, they are going against their faith and everything they supposedly believe in.

This story is important for others to read and know. It shows that we are all equal, not one of us is any better, or any worse than any other person on this earth, regardless of race or culture. If we believe otherwise, we are going against everything our founding fathers strived for, and everything brave lives died for. People need to notice that when it comes down to faith, rights, and basic human good, it doesn't matter whatsoever about the color of our skin, or where we came from. We are all fellow Americans with the same rights and should treat each other as such.

There Were Two Sides of Change, Peaceful and Violent

As we sat down across from each other on Mrs. Nancy's squishy couch with a cup of tea, I couldn't help feeling anticipation for the amazing stories that were to come. Mrs. Rorex was 21 years old when she first really understood what was going on with segregation. Her eyes were opened in September 1957, on her wedding day. She also saw changes where she worked. "Everything started to change. Blacks were put in white schools, the government closed black schools in the early 60s. The kids from black schools weren't as educated because of the lack of funding or proper materials. Then the violence got out of control. The prob-

Interviewer: Claire Carter
Interviewee: Nancy Rorex
Time Period: 1950s
Location: Arkansas
Affected Group: African American
Setting: Workplace

lem was blacks had to be bused into these white neighborhoods. School was very rough when this happened. People actually walked around with their pockets turned inside out so no one would beat them up for what little money they might have. There were two sides of change, peaceful and violent. The government still wasn't in control. In order to vote you had to go to the court house and that was open from nine to five only. No one was going to let a black person off work to vote. Also, a test was made and it was slanted to where a person with a poor education would not pass. That made it to where only the rich could vote.

"When father was a kid (1930), a white girl was killed and stuck in a belfry in town. A black janitor was accused and a group of white men got him and tied him to a truck and dragged him through town till he died." When asked about memories of events that she still remembered clearly, Mrs. Rorex had lots to say. "I remember watching Martin Luther King on the steps of the Washington Monument giving the speech, 'I Have a Dream.' I had a black maid (Bernise) who practically raised me. Bernise came to my wedding and had to sit in the balcony. Only the white guests could sit in front. I had distant relatives I had never even met sit closer to me than Bernise. That was in 1957. Also, my sister received bomb threats for showing a black kid where the cafeteria was. She was a senior in 1957."

When I asked about what she felt, then and now she was quite honest. "I was an unconscious bigot. Not mean or anything violent or strong but I never quite saw them as equals because that was simply how I, and everyone around me, was raised. I never thought to look at those situations from a different or fairer angle. I just never took a stand for blacks when I was young. They couldn't go to the movies or anything like that. I just saw it as a fact of life. My generation was raised to believe whatever our elders told us without a second thought. Later on I got more involved. I helped set up community centers for blacks. I voted to get Orville Faubus out of office. I was a nurse for a while and segregation could be found even in hospitals. Marian Crank drew up and past a bill saying that white and Negro blood was separate. We weren't allowed to use white blood on Negros because others saw it as a waste. We weren't allowed to use black blood on whites either. We ignored such a silly rule."

"I always take the time to correct others opinion now. I had my eyes opened and I hope to have opened a few minds myself since I figured out the truth. Everybody I knew got their eyes opened at last and knew what was wrong. They (the government) changed the fact that court houses were the only place to vote and changed or threw out the stupid laws that treated blacks like dirt. My husband and I took a lot of time to confront our own prejudices."

Coon-Line: Boat Tickets to Africa

L incoln Munro, my great uncle, was born in Fall River, Massachusetts, in 1945. As a young child, he grew up in the midst of most of the Civil Rights Era happenings. Therefore, the ideas he formed about the human race and what each person meant to it formed accordingly. Perhaps as a result, he pursued several professions including a teacher, but has been a psychologist for many years.

When the interview first began, I wasn't really sure how to present my question, so I started out asking what he knew about the Civil Rights Era. He is a man who knows so much about civil rights from every time period that he

Interviewer: Mackie O'Hara
Interviewee: Lincoln Munro
Time Period: 1970s
Location: Maryland
Affected Group: African American
Setting: School

instantaneously began rattling off information about Martin Luther King Jr. and Rosa Parks. Eventually, I was able to explain that I really wanted to know about a personal experience he had. He had several stories to tell and effectively presented them in a letter he sent me:

Dear Mackie,

After our conversation last week, I found my file on Brentwood, MD where Joset and I lived a few doors away from the Brentwood Elementary School where I taught 5th grade.

I made copies for you of: 1) Boat Ticket to Africa that Jesse Stevens, the racist I told you about, handed out to children who walked to school from their own black community nearby. Check out the recipe for "Instant Nigger" on the back. 2) A copy of the 'Congressional Record' that cited the efforts of my class to change the racist mood. 3) An article from *The Washington Post* (Brentwood bordered Washington, DC). This

report was on the heels of the racial violence at the high school in our district.

Mackie, there were some additional points about the stories I told you about on the phone that I would like to share with you. When Jesse Stevens and I were in a face-to-face, "nose-chewing" after I watched him try to intimidate a ten your old black boy sitting on the park lawn, I knew he was a dangerous man. He was rumored to have an arsenal of weapons in his home.

But, he never harassed another kid after that. Bullies are cowards and that's all he was.

The story about the wedding reception at the Capitol Hill club, where the best man, John, was not allowed to enter because he was black, has a good ending too. Joset and I were bridesmaid and usher. When Judy, the bride told us that her father, a Washington high-roller and member of this club, had told John that he could not enter the club, Joset and I were quite upset. We left the wedding reception promptly to go find John at a nearby restaurant. We apologized to Judy and her new husband, Mark, and we left even before the reception line or anything. We found John and his girlfriend and sat with them. He was amazed and appreciated. A half hour later, Judy & Mark walked in. Yep. They left their own wedding reception to join us. Her parents were furious. She thanked Joset and me for doing what we did and giving them the courage to leave, also.

Mackie, I share with you these stories, not to brag, but because there is an important message that young people might fear. When you do the right thing no matter how scary or how much you might be criticized, some times it leads to good things happening. Martin Luther King is most famous for his nonviolent approach to social injustice. It worked. There were thousands of people maybe millions who were inspired to do what we could and change the social injustices in our country. Not just in Alabama and Mississippi or Arkansas, but in Maryland and in our nation's capitol. And that was years after Martin Luther King's wonderful example. The heart of bigotry and racism still beats in this country. Whether it's Mexicans, Arabs, Asians, or blacks, there is still social injustice that needs to be stood up to. It's up to you and your generation to do what you can.

Love, Uncle Link

He explained exactly what was going on in the divided community. There was Brentwood and North Brentwood, North Brentwood was the African-American town primarily. Although most of the town was not racist, the main trouble maker, Jesse Stevens, was able to portray a fear throughout the community. Uncle Link had not been presented with such blatant prejudice in Fall River, but when he saw Jesse Stevens harassing the little African-American boy on the school playground, he knew what he believed in: he believed that all men were created equal and that no person had the right to bully another person, especially a younger person, because of the color of that person's skin.

Everyone seems to have a story about this issue, whether it was something that happened directly to them, or just something they saw, or committed, everyone has a story about the civil rights of African-Americans in America. The interesting thing about this kind of research is that it is so widespread that the information collected by one person will never be the same as the person's next to them. It is in the destruction of people such as Jesse Stevens that our great nation has become what it is today. We are not perfect, but with the help of 5th grade school teachers like Lincoln Munro, we are getting closer and closer to peace. It also shows that the Civil Rights Movement did not end in 1963, as this story took place in 1973, a full decade later.

I always thought that the Civil Rights Movement was something that was just witnessed in the South; however, I have learned over the course of this interview that the North was just as equally effected and that I have a much more direct relation than I ever believed I did.

No Reply

For this memory project I chose to inter-view my grandparents. My grandfather was a sergeant in the Korean War. My grand-mother was a teacher and an information sec-retary. In other countries and in their own communities, my grandparents saw some of the impact of the Civil Rights Movement. I chose my grandparents because they'd always tell me stories from their past jobs and now I can understand what their stories really mean. This interview took place in their home in Miami, Oklahoma, on November 23, 2006.

Interviewer: Jim Curry
Interviewee: John and Jane Doe
Time Period: 1950s
Location: Fort Smith, AR
Affected Group: African American
Setting: Workplace

My first interview was with my grandfa-ther. He was 19 years old when he went to Korea. During his time in the Army he worked with all kinds of peo-ple. At one point they brought in a lot of Puerto Rican and African American soldiers. My grandfather said that his view was that, as long as everyone did their jobs, he treated them all the same. His only bad experience was when he tried to break up a fight between white and Puerto Rican soldiers; one of the Puerto Ricans got mad and hit him with a fire extinguisher. Later, in Germany, the black soldiers had found out that they could live there and not be discriminated against. They didn't want to leave Germany, but the Army brought in a lot of white soldiers and sent the others back to the U.S. When my grand-father returned to Fort Smith, Arkansas, to live, he said he wasn't really affected by the movement, because there were no African Americas living in his area.

My grandmother talked about the 1950s. She was 34 and work-ing at the Chamber of Commerce in Fort Smith, Arkansas. Every time people wrote, asking for information about motels and restaurants to visit while they'd be traveling through Fort Smith, my grandmother would send them brochures. One day a letter arrived asking, "What motels in Fort Smith are available to a Negro Family?" She asked her

boss about it, he sad, "Nothing is available to Negroes. Do not reply."
She thought that was awful and she felt sick about it.

She went to an African American Methodist minister that she'd
known for several years. Their two churches had worked on youth
projects together. She talked to him about raising money to buy an
old motel and fix it up. That preacher talked with an African
American lawyer and they were eventually able to raise the money.
They bought a motel, remodeled it, and made sure it was available to
black families.

Another experience my grandmother had was after she had married my grandfather. They had stopped at a diner while on a road trip
and went inside. Inside a black family was seated but had not been
served. When my grandparents sat down a waitress quickly came and
asked them for their order. My grandmother said, "Oh. They were
here first," pointing to the black family. "Oh. They can wait," the waitress responded. My grandmother was appalled and said, "No, they
can't and we won't bother waiting either," and then left the diner.

My views of my grandparents didn't change, but the interviews
made me see even more what people had gone through. I also saw
how fair my grandparents were. My grandmother's last comment
was, "I just hope that today's young African Americans know and
appreciate what their parents and grandparents went through."

Fight for Respect

My Big Momma, Cornelious Walker, was a woman of great stature and beauty. She is such an intelligent woman who had great hopes and dreams, some weren't completed because of the lack of money; but she tried her best, which made me love her even more. I interviewed her at her home in Little Rock, Arkansas. This occurred on the 24th of November. This was the best person for me to interview, because she has experienced a lot in her lifetime. The more I know about her, the closer I feel to my Big Momma.

Interviewer:	Alexandria Gordon
Interviewee:	Cornelious Walker
Time Period:	1950s
Location:	Jefferson County, AR
Affected Group:	African American
Setting:	Restaurant

Born in Jefferson County on December 11, 1929, she had encountered a lot because she was born in the South. Most of the things weren't beautiful sights to see. With a mind to learn she learned to understand the ways of others. She didn't always agree, but she handled them. Being born in the South impacted her life in both negative and positive ways. One negative way was that society had her believing that the white man was evil, which wasn't true about all of the whites. On the other hand the blacks were also led to believe that they were (expletive deleted) and colored people, but hey everybody has a color whether it is purple, green, or blue. African Americans deserved equal rights and respect as much as everyone else. She realized that whatever you want, you must work hard for it because no one is going to just give it to you. There is a little good in every race because through the skin color we are blessed with different personalities. That is what makes our world amazing.

Around the age of 26, my Big Momma worked in a restaurant. During this time there was a lot of racism going on between mostly the blacks and whites. Blacks had to eat in the back, but the whites were always eating in the front. If you were black and worked there, you had to work in the back. Whether you were black or white, everyone ate the food you prepared. The only reason why my Big Momma put up with this was because she had a family to provide for.

One day, she had enough. My Big Momma began to proclaim, "If you white honkies are good enough to eat the food I cook, then I should be able to sit where I want to. I believe I have earned that right." She said this to her boss, because he had told her that when she was on her break, she can go stand outside in the back. She refused this because she was tired and felt that if you can let whites eat in then so could she. She grabbed a knife out of her pocket and said, "I Quit! I refuse to be disrespected as long as I am alive. I have put up with this too long, now it is my turn for this to end." She walked out the front door past all the whites with her head held high. As she left, a man called her a stupid black (expletive deleted). She ran up to him with the knife and said "Are you ready to die? If not then leave me alone you honkey." He left her alone because he found out that not every black person is going to take his mess. This taught her that you couldn't always talk to solve your problems. Sometimes you have to stoop to their level.

On a bright day in the store, my Big Momma beat the breaks off three policemen. She did this when she was about 42 years old. She has always been buff and stocky so you knew if you bothered her or her seven kids, you had a whopping coming. A policeman had grabbed my dad when he was about eight years old and accused him of stealing. My Big Momma had just turned around after paying for her stuff, and became enraged at the sight. He tried to call for back up, because my Big Momma was beating the breaks off the man. When the other police arrived, she was knocking them down left and right as quick as they came. My dad just watched because, what can a little eight year old kid do? She went to jail overnight, not a very long time for how she reacted. She got lucky. God had to have been watching her that day. She had learned that if you fight, choose who you fight carefully because there will be consequences to pay.

Now that she is older, she is much wiser, but still has that powerful punch. The surprising thing about all of this is that she is 74 and gets along with everyone no matter what their race. Also, now that we have a mixed family, everyone loves each other and gets along.

Respect lies in the heart and with people who surround you. She also has the effort to give the respect.

I learned that fighting doesn't always solve everything because of this project. Also, respect is the best thing you can ask for and to give to others. I learned that my Big Momma didn't play then and doesn't play now. So stay on her good side because when you mess up, she doesn't respect you anymore. The only way to get it back, is to get it like everything else in life, you have to earn it.

Children Do Not Know

Patricia Faye Brooks grew up in Pine Bluff, Arkansas. She traveled with her grandmother to Washington D.C. She really was not aware of racism until she was actually a teenager. She is currently a counselor and lives in Little Rock, Arkansas.

Interviewer: Amanda McClendon
Interviewee: Patricia Faye Brooks
Time Period: 1950s
Location: Pine Bluff, AR
Affected Group: African American
Setting: Restaurant

The interview was, at first, just a simple assignment and then became something more: a doorway to the past through my interviewee's eyes. Her childhood took place in the time where major events took place, such as the Montgomery Bus Boycott, *Brown v. Board of Education*, the integration of Little Rock Central High School, and many other significant events that changed and shaped the civil rights of Americans.

The memory that stuck out of Patricia's mind happened when she was five and still naive to racism. She said that she and her mother were out shopping. Then she told her mother that she wanted to shop by herself. Her mother said okay and walked off. Little did Patricia know that her mother was just standing by a nearby pole watching her the whole time. After her mom walked off, Patricia decided to sit at the counter and buy a coke. She put her money on the counter and then waited. The waitress was at the other end and stood there and did not move. Then, a man came and stood by her. Soon her mom came and told her it was time to go. Patricia told her mom that she wanted to buy a coke, but the lady did not move. Her mother said the woman was lazy and did not want to do her job. Later on in her teenage years, in recollection of the incident, her mother told her that she was standing by the pole giving the lady, I-dare-you-to-make-my-daughter-move stare. That is why the man came and stood by her to make sure nothing happened.

All parents wanted to do was to shelter and to protect their children from racism. I was taught that you should not do this or do that and it was never questioned. She realized about this when she was younger and she saw the image on television where they were hosing the blacks and using dogs. She made a comment to her mother, "I'm glad Arkansas isn't like that." Her mother replied, "I've really sheltered you."

Racism is something that is taught, everyone knows that. It is not a disease and no one is born with it. It is a state of mind; people are afraid of what they do not know about. Different races, in my opinion, fear each other and do not know much about each other, so they judge the race before knowing the culture. For many years, people have struggled with the harsh realities of this world, and racism is one of them. Many people have battled for the civil rights of people. Even today, racism is swept under the rug, and is seen in public places, and even in government. Patricia said, "There are laws that protect us from it, but it's hidden."

I think that today, we could overcome racism by getting to know the different races before judging them. We are all created equal. If someone got to know the cultures and characteristics from a person of a different ethnicity, they would learn a lot on how similar and interesting they are.

This interview opened my eyes to racism through a different point. It made me realize it is something that is really taught. I recall my father always telling me that one of the cutest memories he has of me is when I was in pre-school and I would refer to my classmates as the "purple boy," or the "blue girl." He asked me why they were purple, blue, or whatever color I had labeled them as. My reply was, "Because Daddy, the purple boy had on a purple shirt." This is a prime example through personal experience, that no one knows about the different race and racism until they are taught it, or come to the age of realization and see the world for what it really is.

Struggle for a Better America

The time was 8:45 p.m. on a Tuesday evening. I was sitting in a wooden chair. Across the dining room table sat Harish Patel, facing toward me looking eager to start sharing information. In the background, we could hear a parakeet chirping. Dr. Patel, my dad, had gotten home from work and was in his business attire. He seemed relaxed, however, even after coming home from work. I was about to start asking questions.

Interviewer: Aashka Patel
Interviewee: Harish Patel
Time Period: 1990s
Location: Georgia
Affected Group: Indian American
Setting: Neighborhood

Harish Patel had moved to the United States in 1991. He said that in the past 15 years he has been living in America, he has seen a lot of change in racial issues. He believes that, as Americans, we have become more liberal in the sense that people of different races get along better and are accepted more in society. He then told of discrimination he and some of his friends have faced due to the color of their skin.

The main setting of his stories was in a town called Gainesville that is located in the outskirts of Atlanta, Georgia. "Gainesville," Dr. Patel said, "was inhabited by almost 100% white citizens." At this point in the interview he talked with a normal voice. He also said that it was very uncommon to find an African-American or any other race besides Caucasian in that town. The first experience of which he told was when he went to a restaurant in Gainesville. Dr. Patel said that he felt that he was not treated as well as other customers in the restaurant. He said that the other people made him feel out of place, as if he didn't belong there. After this experience, he never went to Gainesville again.

Another experience he told of was what happened to one of his friends in Gainesville, Georgia. At this point in the interview, Dr. Patel's voice started getting quieter. One of his really close friends bought a shop in Gainesville from the previous owner, who was

Caucasian. After people came to know that an Indian couple had bought it, they stopped purchasing goods and eventually stopped coming. The citizens of Gainesville boycotted the store in a non-physical way. After just a few months, the couple had to sell the store on account that no one would buy anything from it because they were not white.

"Experiences of this sort were more common back then than they are now," Dr. Patel said. However, he continued, just that very same day he had walked into the Bank of America. There was a receptionist at the door asking what they had come for and then told them to wait. After Dr. Patel told the man what he was there for, he was asked to sit on the couch and was told that the receptionist would call him when they were ready. A few minutes later, however, an elderly Caucasian couple walked through the door. They told the receptionist what they needed and he told them to sit down and wait. He offered them tea, juice and cookies while Dr. Patel was sitting right next to them. The receptionist did not ask him if he wanted anything to eat or drink. This action was obviously taken because the receptionist had something against Indian people or people of different races in general. Dr. Patel said, "I regret not asking the receptionist right there why he did not offer me juice." He said that he would write a letter to Bank of America explaining what had happened that day and he wanted to know why this action was taken. Dr. Patel finished, however, by saying, "Although I have experienced racism in today's time, it has gotten a lot better since the first time I came to America."

These stories stick in my mind because it tells of interesting experiences I have never heard my dad talk about. His stories tell about the hard times he and some of his friends have had in the past fifteen years due to the color of their skin. I would have never thought that such a small thing such as an owner of a store who is not Caucasian would cause a boycott on a store. These stories stick in my mind also because of the fact that I have not been discriminated against like this; it makes me wonder how bad it would have been 50 years ago. These stories are of great importance to me and show me how life was like for people of different races 15 years ago.

These stories have to do with the struggle for civil rights in America in many ways. It shows that over the years changes have occurred in the sense that racism is now less commonly seen. Discrimination is not completely wiped out, but it has become scarcer than what it has been over the course of the last 50 years when civil rights had just started. It's true that America is slowly becoming better when it comes to the rights of its citizens of all races.

But I'm Cuban, Not Mexican

Looking around my grandmother and step-grandfather's living room, I see tons of pictures of their children and grandchildren. Sitting on the coffee table is a picture of my mom, my brother, and me from our church two years. Next to me on the couch, wearing a button-up flannel shirt tucked into his blue jeans and a huge smile on his tan wrinkled face under snow white hair, is my step-grandfather, Carlos A. Lopez.

Interviewer: Jennifer Thompson
Interviewee: Carlos A. Lopez
Time Period: 1950s
Location: New Mexico
Affected Group: Hispanic American
Setting: Store

Carlos was born in Havana, Cuba. He grew up there until the Communists began to take control of Cuba. Public buildings were being bombed around his home and his environment was becoming more and more dangerous. Over time, one million Cubans evacuated to escape from the violence caused by the Communist uprising. In 1954, he and his mother decided to evacuate too, and moved to America, where his two sisters were living. One sister lived in New Mexico, and the other lived in Florida. He moved to Albuquerque, New Mexico, took classes part time at the University of New Mexico, and joined the Air Force there. He lived on the Air Force base, and everywhere he traveled he was exposed to racism.

Throughout the interview Carlos discussed how he had moved to America to escape Fidel Castro's reign in Cuba. When he arrived in New Mexico, he found that there were racist feelings between whites and browns (or Hispanics) not just between whites and blacks. He shared how anyone with a Latino name or even looked Latino was labeled a Mexican, and how this ignorance angered him almost as much as the discrimination against him.

Once, when passing through a bus stop in a Southern state, Carlos saw a store with a sign in the window saying, "No Blacks or Mexicans." He tried to enter the store because, being Cuban, the sign did not apply to him. When he entered the store, the manager asked him what he thought he was doing.

"Did you read the sign?" the store manager asked.

"Yes," answered Carlos, "But I'm Cuban, not Mexican."

"It doesn't matter, it's the same thing. Get out of here," the man replied.

Carlos's voice dropped as he told me this, and it was obvious that this story from fifty years ago still bothered him today.

Carlos learned a lot from this experience. Although he was serving in the United States' Air Force, people still felt the need to judge him because of his skin color. Right after the incident, Carlos was angry. Coming from Cuba, this discrimination was new and unfair to him. Then, Carlos began to be frightened because police and other authority figures also had this attitude toward him. Luckily, the University of New Mexico was a fairly liberal college, and he did not have to deal with as much discrimination there as he would have elsewhere. He was also able to make friends with many other Latinos, giving him a sense of security. Later in life, Carlos decided to become a Presbyterian minister. Through his education to become a minister he learned much more about discrimination and how to peacefully react to it. Today, Carlos realizes that discrimination is caused by ignorance and stereotypes. It is through this knowledge that Carlos feels education will help people finally overcome racism.

When many people think of the Civil Rights Movement, they think of the struggle for African American's rights. However, this story shows that many races have had to struggle and are still struggling for civil rights. People come to this country to chase their dreams, to accomplish things that are impossible in their own country, to receive a greater education, or, like Carlos, to escape from violence in their own country. However, in the past, America has not always welcomed these people with open arms. Like Carlos, many people were discriminated against and were forced to live in fear of people who thought their race is superior to others. Instead of giving up, Carlos continued to live in the United States, became a Presbyterian minister, and in the early 1990's, married my grand mother, a white woman. His story is a great example that stereotypes can be overcome, and "liberty and justice for all" can eventually be achieved.

History through an interview like this may not be as easy to comprehend as a textbook, but it is much easier to relate to. To think that the person you are talking to has had a first-hand or second-hand experience with racism is very moving. While their experiences may not have made front page news, like Rosa Parks', every story helped shape America's civil rights into what they are today. Some stories have positive effects, and some stories have negative effects. But without all of these stories, we would not know how far we have come, or how far we have left to go.

Behind the Counter

My name is Meaghan Karney, and I attend Little Rock Central High School. I am in the class of 2012 in Coach Johnson's Civic's class. I have interviewed my mother, JoAnn Karney, who told stories of my grandmother (her mother), Muriel Yolanda Sosa Heffner and my grandfather, J. C. Heffner.

Muriel Heffner was born on June 24, 1925. Her husband, who was eleven years older than her, was in the military (Army) so she moved around a lot. In fact, after they started dating (initially going out on a blind date that her boss had set up in New York City), he was transferred to Tokyo, Japan, so she put in for a transfer with her government job as well. It all became history from then on. She had three kids: Linda Heffner, JoAnn Karney (my mother), and Leslie Schwager. My grandmother worked at the Rolex Watch Company, which was located at the Empire State building in New York City, as an administrative assistant for a government agency in New York and at the USDA Food and Nutrition Service as a Food Stamp Program manager. My grandmother was 100% Spanish (her mother was from Puerto Rico and her father was from Cuba) and was a housewife for eighteen years after marrying my grandfather.

Interviewer: Meaghan Karney
Interviewee: JoAnn Karney
Time Period: 1960s
Location: California/Texas
Affected Group: African American
Setting: Public

The following is an interview of my grandmother, Muriel, told by my mother, JoAnn:

Q: **How old were you and where were you living when the changes in civil rights started happening? Were you in school, or working, or doing something else?**

A: I believe you are referring to that period of time when there were reform movements in the United States which were aimed at stopping racial discrimination, right? That period of time seemed to be around 1955 until the late 1960s, say around 1968 or so. My mother, Muriel Yolanda Sosa was actually living in Death Valley, California, at the time having her eldest daughter. She was 30 years old. My Dad, J. C. Heffner, was stationed in the Army there. My mother was at home with her newborn daughter, but she remembers her husband getting called out a lot to help out the National Guard keep order in various parts of the state. She also remembers that the blacks and white stayed apart, and she never really mingled with any of the black people, and never had any friend of African American descent. She lived on base in a predominately white area of the base while the black people lived in their own area. It was very segregated and at the time, she took it for granted and never was given the opportunity to mingle with any black people for fear that she would be hurt or be an outcast. She definitely noticed that black people were treated differently.

Q: **What kinds of changes did you see happening where you lived? Were they happening to you or to someone in your family or to someone else you knew?**

A: During this time period, my parents were transferred to Munich, Germany, where they had me, and then on to San Francisco, California, where they had my youngest sister. My Dad retired from the Army in 1996 and moved down to Texas. My mom really didn't remember segregation going on in Germany as I believe this may have been more of a United States issue. There may have been a little bit going on, but not to the extent it was happening in the United States during this time period. I do remember my Dad being called to help the National Guard in the Watts riots in Los Angeles, California, during the summer of 1965. We were living in San Francisco at the time, and he took the entire family with him. We stayed at my grandparent's house (Meaghan's great grandparents), who lived close to Los Angeles. I remember the television was on the entire time, and I remember seeing fires and police everywhere. I also remember the sirens going on through the night. It was very scary, and my Dad was down there in the middle of it all.

The riots began in August of 1965 in Watts, which was a suburb of Los Angeles. A white California Highway Patrol motorcycle officer had pulled over a black person who [he] believed was intoxicated due to his erratic driving. This person also did not pass the sobriety tests, so he was arrested. The police did not let this person's brother drive the car home, and the police had it impounded. Then the mobs started to form, and riots broke out. There was a lot of damage from looting, fighting, and vandalism. Stores were set on fire. Most of the damage was to white-owned businesses as they were said to have caused resentment in this predominately black area of town. The riots resulted from a build up of racial tension that had been going on in the area for some time.

The riots lasted for six days, and my dad was called down there to help keep order. This was a big change occurring in our part of the United States, and me being only eight years old at the time, didn't even really understand what was going on, but I remember my parents being very upset about the whole ordeal, and my grandparents were mad and seemed to be very biased against black people probably because of the time period they had grown up in.

Q: Do you remember particular events or experiences that have stayed with you? When and where did this happen? Who all was involved? Do you remember particular things that people said or wrote? What happened...how did it start and how did it end?

A: I remember a couple of events that happened to my mom during this time period. The first was after my dad retired and moved to Texas. We were living in a cramped apartment on the second floor. There was this black family living directly underneath us. They would play their stereo into the wee hours of the morning, and we could never get any sleep. After pounding on the walls several times and jumping on the floor, it just got louder and louder and went on all night long. I remember my mom taking the initiative to go to the first floor and talk with this family. I also remember that she was already biased because of their color, and she told us to wish her good luck. Well, to make a long story short, it was found out that there was no insulation between the apartments, and that every time we walked or played cars on the floor, they could hear all the thumping noises we were making, so they were just trying to block it out with the loud music.

They turned out to be the most awesome family, and their oldest daughter and my youngest sister became best friends for life. All of my family's prejudices seemed to be wiped away at that moment. In fact, the father of that family walked my youngest sister down the aisle in 1996 at her wedding since our dad has passed away. And 43 years later, we are still in touch with them. Also, right after we moved out of those apartments, we bought a house in the same area. This family bought a house around the corner from us. I will never forget that there was a family next door to them who showed a lot of racial prejudice and insisted our friends move. In fact, they tried to get a court order to make it happen saying it was a "white" neighborhood only. They couldn't get them to move, so in order to make a statement, instead of linking up their back fence to our black friend's fence that had already been built, they built an entire new fence right along the fence they already had so there was a "double fence" between their houses. This really hurt my parents to see what was being done to their best friends at the time.

The second event and the most memorable event that my mom was seeing and experiencing at the time was when she was a program maganer for the USDA Food and Nutrition Service. She would travel to various small neighborhood grocery stores within the state of Texas to make sure that the store owners were complying with the Food Stamp policies set up by the government. This would be to ensure that things weren't being purchased with food stamps that were not on the approved list. Some of those things were candy and cigarettes. She had stopped in a small grocery store in a small town in Texas, and noticed that there were two gentlemen waiting in line, one white and one black. They both had a pack of cigarettes, and they were both trying to purchase them with food stamps. The grocery store clerk "behind the counter," who was white, allowed the white man to purchase his with food stamps, but not the black man.

My mom had to confront the grocery store owner as well as the clerk. She was afraid that they kept a gun behind the counter, and they would harm her for the confrontation. They gave her no explanation as to why they did this other than "the white man was one of them." My mom told them that rules were rules, and they shouldn't be broken just because of someone's prejudices. My mom was very angry, but she had to keep her temper under control. Also, she had to do a follow up visit on that store to make sure they were going to comply or they would not be able to accept the food stamps in the future. Her follow up visits with that particular store showed that they began to comply with the laws of not allowing anyone, whether black or white, to purchase "forbidden" things with food stamps. Now whether they did this because they got rid of their prejudices or whether they did this because they did not want to lose their ability to accept food stamps is still left to be known.

Q: **How did you feel at the time it was happening? What did you do? How did you feel about it later? Have you thought about it much since you've grown older?**

A: My mother was very upset about what had happened earlier at the grocery store because she had overcome her racial prejudices earlier on as was evidenced by her life long friends who were African-American. She does remember her biases against black people before that apartment situation occurred and also her strong biases when her husband had to go protect Watts, CA during the riots, so she did understand where these people were coming from although she had hoped they would be more receptive and change their views just like she had done. She was very shocked that discrimination against blacks was still happening in certain parts of the country. She did confront the grocery clerk and the store manager and let them know what was going on, and she felt like maybe she had made some headway with them, or at least she had tried. She always felt she had done the right thing in confronting the store manager and the clerk, both for her job in making them comply with the food stamp law and also to make them be aware of their racial biases.

Q: How did this experience change people you knew? How did it change you? Did it affect you in any choices or situations you were in later in your life?

A: The first experience at the apartment changed people around my mom to become more accepting of people who were not of their same race. I also changed the way in which this African American couple viewed white people because they didn't seem so timid or afraid anymore that they were not going to be accepted by other races. They saw that since my mom was willing to extend a "friendly hand," they were willing to do the same without having to fear rejection. The second experience not only opened the eyes of the store clerk and manager to their prejudices, but also, [it led to] the African-American man—that my mom spoke up for—[being] very grateful to her for not being biased against him. Both of these situations changed my mom forever which also had influences that were passed down to us and our children. We never judged people according to their color. To us, everyone is the same on the inside. My mom became the same way in never being judgmental toward anyone. After all, being Spanish, she was also a minority race and had to deal with some of the very same issues of people being prejudiced toward her. I think the attitude that she received from all of this was the driving force behind her friendship with this African American couple for the past 43 years. In fact, she calls this friend her sister!

I have learned so much from this interview with my mother. I learned things about my grandmother and things about racial problems that I never would have known if it were not for this interview. I learned that back in the day, people would act illegally just to not show respect to the African Americans. It is crazy to me that they would go through all of that trouble just to make known that they did not like them. This has made my relationship with my grandma closer; even though she has Alzheimer's which is why she could not do this interview with me. I wish I could talk to her about all the things I learned about her past because I know she would have a lot more details to add on all of it. I have learned a lot in this interview and I hope to learn more about the civil rights movement as I became older because I think it is a very important part of history.

I Was Always for Desegregation

We are sitting in the grand room of a two bedroom house. Behind my grandfather are floor-to-ceiling shelves decorated and covered with artifacts from every corner of the world. Among the array of cultural and priceless souvenirs are pictures of family: old, new, black and white, people I know and people I am clueless of. Some dating back way past the days I've seen. Some pictures are of places my grandfather and deceased grandmother have visited all across continents far from home. I sit on the couch across the room from the single-winged chair my grandfather rests in. I can't help but wonder what has happened within the

Interviewer: Lindsey Garland
Interviewee: Dr. John Forrest Henry Jr.
Time Period: 1950s
Location: Little Rock, AR
Affected Group: White
Setting: Workplace

years of 1917 and 2008 that has allowed, prevented, and challenged my grandparents to visit all these places. What wars, riots, and boycotts made it possible, or impossible, to search the earth. But I mostly wonder what change could have occurred between the times of priceless black and white pictures, to the world I know today.

My grandfather looks like the typical grandfather. Tall, with white hair, a button-up shirt, black slacks, and black dress shoes. He's lived to reach 90 years of age and is very healthy looking despite the years life has worn onto him. He's wearing a smile that's ear-to-ear and glasses designed as anyone would expect of a grandparent. He's a very accomplished man. I haven't known him but 15 years of his almost century-long life, but something about him gives me a sense of confidence, pride, and contentment with his life. I also see something else in him: anxiety. The anxious look on his face is somewhat confusing to me. I can't tell if this anxiety is good or bad. Might he be afraid to face the past? Or possibly thrilled to share his, theirs, and our stories? The story of what was, what did, and what has changed and shaped

America to the "freedom-land' it is today. What did he do to change the world? What didn't he do? Where did he stand in the conflict of color, morality, and integration? Who is the man he is today?

My main purpose in this interview was to get to know my grandfather, who in my eyes, has lived to see a change in everything. I think about my life, the way my life has always been, and I try to think about it flipped, turned, and tossed into a world where color in school was more than a bubble on a standardized test. The most suitable to teach me a history lesson about segregation, integration, and the process of getting from and to it is my grandfather. He is a living, breathing, talking history book. So who better to interview in hopes to catch a glimpse of the past than a man who was there?

One story in particular sticks in my mind. The story of segregation in the one place that seems the most unimaginable.

My grandfather, who was a physician, worked at Baptist Hospital. He walked from his home at 23 Maryland, which was located near Woodrow before it was torn down, to work each morning. Every day as he would enter the hospital, the one place where I would have assumed to be completely desegregated, he would enter through the white waiting room. I was confused as to whether it was the hospitals or just the waiting rooms that were segregated. "They [blacks and whites] went to the same hospital, but they went to different parts… it's really hard to imagine that if you were colored you got admitted to the basement." A hospital segregated? A place where life and death are always on the line and a place where nothing is supposed to impact your treatment. I just can't stop thinking about that.

As things such as schools, restaurant, water fountains, restrooms, and buses started integrating, the waiting rooms did as well. When I asked him when the waiting rooms became desegregated, he responded, "After Cosgrove Jr. came, he still wanted them segregated, but I insisted we didn't." I'm not quite sure who this Cosgrove Jr. is, but what I got of this one simple sentence was that my grandfather assisted in resolving the segregation of hospitals. He assisted in resolving segregation period.

Now, curious as to where he stood in this war of colors, I asked what he believed about the whole situation. I assumed, after his last sentence, that he was for desegregation. "I was always for it [desegregation]." I also asked him how this experience changed him. "The only way it changed me was I could be more open about the way I felt."

The reasons why this story sticks in my head are countless and somewhat confusing. First off, hospitals are a place where I assumed equality was always a given. Because life is life and color, gender, creed, religion, even financial security should never affect your treatment. Secondly, I saw a side of my grandfather that I had always wondered about. He said, "The only way it changed me was I could be more open about the way I felt." As long as I have known my grandfather, as many unforgettable stories I've heard, I've never heard him speak passionately on a controversial topic. Right after he said that it never changed him, he said something I don't agree with: "I've learned don't argue with friends on politics and religion." The reason I don't agree with his thought is because if one person had just stayed quiet and not argued, my historical school may still be the segregated hate-hole it was 50 years ago. He said that it didn't change him, and of all the years I've known him, I've known him as the same man. And no doubt he is a good, charitable, man, but to know that before it was "right" or "cool" to stand up for the right thing, he was doing it, that makes me look up to him in an indescribable way.

The main reason this story should be read and saved is to show a side to a story most people today don't know about; that a white, successful, man with two children in the Little Rock School District, was for desegregation. I've been taught just to assume that because of my race and lifestyle, it would have been normal for me to be the type of person in every segregation documentary with a hateful face and negative demeanor. I think this story shows that no person, no matter what race, should be assumed to believe in any particular thing.

I learned so much from this experience. The most surprising was that, as my grandfather put it, "Most of us were for it [de-segregation]. A lot of people changed, but a lot of them didn't, some of them are just as adamant today." Most of "us" were for it? Assuming most means the Caucasians at the time, that is surprising in and of itself. In my class this year, we've watched countless documentaries, read several articles, even talked with people who lived during the civil rights movement and not one of these gave me the impression that "most" Caucasians were for de-segregation. It's not as surprising as it is reassuring.

So much can be learned from this interview. It shows so much diversity from the cliché stories we hear over and over. The interviews we are used to seeing are your average older man with anger in his voice and still yearning for forgiveness for his past. This is simply a granddaughter asking her grandfather about what he knows, what's he's been through, but mostly, what he's changed. None of the interviews I've seen have asked such a simple question as "what have you done." They all seem to be pointing the finger at someone else and blaming another race. This is different because my grandfather didn't just live the history and see the history; he was part of the change in the history. That's something that separated this interview from others: its simplicity.

Did Not Affect Me Very Much

The person I decided to interview for my Central High Memory Project was my grandfather. I chose my grandfather because he grew up before, during, and after the Civil Rights Movement. He would be able to give me experiences throughout this time in our nation's history. My grandfather gave me views on racism from a child's view and gave me the perspective of a white southern male's outlook on the Civil Rights Movement.

Interviewer: Adam Thannisch
Interviewee: Thomas Walton
Time Period: 1950s
Location: Mississippi
Affected Group: African American
Setting: School

When the interview began, I asked, "How old were you, and where were you were living when the changes in civil rights started happening? Were you in school, working, or doing something else?" My grandfather responded by answering all the questions. He said he was living in Mississippi working at a plywood production plant. As he continued to explain I asked if he saw many changes. To me his response was of great surprise, he said he was not greatly affected by the outcome of the Civil Rights Movement.

I then came to two important topics I thought people would be interested in: segregation in the army, and a "White Council" as my grandfather told what it was. I had just finished my basic interview questions when I asked my first of these questions. I asked how he saw segregation in the Army. He replied in short answers, not really showing effort to elaborate. He said that there were all black units, which were led by white officers. I had already heard of this, from the Civil War. The next question was about the "White Council." He stated that one of his college friends had formed such a council. I then discovered that he was a part of the group. He mentioned that it was a group who opposed desegregation of the country. After asking these two questions, I was very interested in what else my grandfather had to say.

I then moved onto questions that involved my grandfather on a more personal level. I asked if at the time of the Civil Rights

Movement was he for or against it. It seemed to me he tried avoiding it by saying that he was raised on beliefs that it shouldn't happen. He never took a direct stand on either side. I then asked whether or not my grandfather had any relations with African Americans. "In Yazoo, Mississippi," he said, "I grew up living an alley away from the black part of town." He mentioned that he was friends with some of the younger African American children. I then moved onto his parents and their views. My grandfather said that his dad was dead long before the Civil Rights Movement. He said that even though his family was raised to think that desegregation was bad, they did not care. I then asked about how his coworkers saw the movement. My grandfather said that nearly all of them were against it. Then he added that most of the South was against it. After all of this, I asked did he see any acts of racism to people besides African American, and in his short answers he said no.

I learned a lot from interviewing my grandfather. This project has shown me a side of my grandfather I would have never known, thus helping me see him for who he was and who he is. My views toward the Civil Rights Movement have not changed, but the ones of my grandfather did. The one answer that shocked me the most was his reply on if the Civil Rights Movement affected his life. He said that it did not affect him much afterwards. To me this was important because it showed me that people who did not want desegregation or for the Civil Rights Movement to succeed were people who made it a part of their lives.

I Still Don't Understand to This Day

I have never been so astounded in my life as I was when I discovered my grandfather had actually lived before I was born. I had never thought to ask him about his past, never questioned what he had seen, never even realized he had lived through such crucial periods in American history, even though I knew he was almost eighty. I didn't realize this until I walked up to him one day and asked him one simple question: "Granddad, what do you know about the Civil Rights Movement?" After twenty minutes straight of jaw-dropping details, all I could think to do was to grab a tape recorder and head back to his quiet house in the suburbs of Little Rock, Arkansas, to learn straight from the horse's mouth about how it actually felt to live through the struggle that brought every American to his feet.

Interviewer:
Brenna Gilstrap

Interviewee:
Bill Gilstrap

Time Period:
1930s-1940s

Location:
Mississippi

Affected Group:
African American

Setting:
Military

My grandfather was born and raised in Mississippi in a family that never spoke much about Civil Rights. His great grandfather was a general in the Confederate army, and his grandmother shared Confederate views, but around his fourth grade year, my grandfather decided he did not. Most of his experiences occurred while he was in the air force, monitoring the main issues in the country as they came.

The purpose of this interview was to find out exactly what it felt like, what it was like, to live in the Civil Rights era. One cannot get the full feel of history from a textbook; it takes more than that to understand what truly happened and the impact that it made. These generations, so ripe with memories of events that rocked the very foundation of the country, sadly cannot be within reach forever. This interview not only brought me closer to my grandfather, but allowed me to see through his eyes this period that holds so much history in America, especially in my home town.

There was one story in particular that my grandfather told me which stuck in my mind. It occurred when he was in the Air Force. He was sitting with a few of his coworkers while they discussed the ruling that outlawed separate but equal schools. One of the gentlemen in the room began ranting about equality and segregation. What caught my grandfather's attention was when he went so far as to say, "Why, blacks, they aren't even human!" Everyone turned to the black recruit in the room with him. They say it took several men to keep him from tearing the man who made the comment apart.

This experience never has rested well with my grandfather. His problem was, as has been mine, trying to figure out where any man could get the notion that he was better than another man because of the color of his skin. He said he never understood how anyone could justify enslaving a race, or accusing a man same as he of not even being human. How any person could rationalize it was beyond him, and he keeps that thought with him every day: that every man is equal, and it makes no sense to say otherwise.

This experience of my grandfather's just showed how America felt, how America was, during that day and age. It gives a taste of the mentality that possessed almost every man, except for those that couldn't just be told something, that had to know why first and then remember what later. He says that his generation is still fighting the battle.

A woman approached him in church talking about how God segregated the races by color for a reason. He said he believed every man to be equal in God's eyes, and she responded by saying, "Oh, you're one of them, aren't you?"

The sad truth is that the old prejudice stays within some people today. They were raised in a world that taught them to think that blacks were second-class citizens, and segregation was justified. To this day some possess the idea that there isn't racial equality in the world, and it is my opinion that living out the dream my grandfather has always had of an equal world with equal rights will help to let the old thoughts pass, and a sane world where 'liberty and justice for all' actually exist.

Equality in the Navy

My grandfather, Max "Kermit" Livingston, served in the Navy during the heated times of the Korean War. He was a naval aviator and fought in many of the important battles of the war. At the same time, he realized that integration was becoming a large part in the Navy and the other armed forces and that he would have to come to terms with the other races.

Interviewer:
Livingston
Anderson

Interviewee:
Max "Kermit"
Livingston

Time Period:
1950s

Location:
Korea

Affected Group:
African American

Setting:
Military

The interview took place at my grandfather's house in Little Rock. I can hear the rain splashing against the window and the occasional sounds of thunder. The large living room was filled with the oriental rugs and small trinkets of my grandparent's worldwide travel. On a large wooden table there is a large assortment of nutcrackers hand made in Germany. There is a large wooden grandfather clock that rings on the hour with an ominous hum.

My grandfather was wearing a blue polo and a pair of khaki pants as he had just come from church. He has brownish/grayish hair and is tall. He was always friendly and never seemed to have a bad day. He always had a good joke to tell and if you ever met him, it was like you had known him forever. He is extremely kind and generous and gives to the poor and donates money to charitable organizations.

He was born in Kansas and attended high school. After graduating he went to college then joined the Navy. He became a naval aviator and while there was no war going on, he flew training missions and towed target airplanes for ship based anti aircraft gunners. But as soon as the Korean War broke out, he found himself escorting bombers and going on raids. Kermit was stationed on an aircraft carrier and flew Corsairs and other propeller, driven aircraft as jets were not yet available. He retired afterwards and became a commercial pilot for Delta Airlines.

My grandfather noticed that African Americans and people of other races were being stationed on the carrier and a lot of white sailors and airmen were not taking it so well. He remembered that pranks and cruel jokes were played on the African Americans and on one occasion one person was nearly knocked overboard. One occasion, he remembered there was a black officer on the ship and my grandfather and his friends had to salute him which was strange to all of them as they had never had to do it before. He also remembered that a Special Forces team that was on the ship after an operation and he saw that several members of the team were African Americans and that instead of being shunned from the group they were accepted in their team.

My grandfather mostly kept to himself and did not get involved but eventually made friends with an African American deckhand who had been put on the ship after his training. My grandfather recalled one event when a damaged fighter was forced to belly land on the carrier after being heavily damaged. He remembered that the plane slid into the side of the bridge and caused a large fire and at once sailors of all races rushed to save the pilot and put out the fire. He said he saw several white sailors drag a wounded black sailor out of harms way and several black sailors help rescue the pilot from his burning plane. He also remembered while escorting bombers to a site where there was heavy fighting a soldier on the ground made the call that they needed air support and they were all surprised to hear that the man was black. It also pleased him to hear that they were able to take charge and make life-saving decisions. Before long, he and his friends began to hang out with the African American sailors and before long they were good friends. He also saw that officers were treating African American and soldiers of different races with more respect.

That story stuck in my mind because I always was interested in the military and how soldiers would react to integration the armed forces.

In the end of the interview I was happy to have spoken with my Grandfather regarding the integration of the military during the Korean War. And today, soldiers of all races can fight together without the worry of being separated because the color of their skin.

Chapter Four:
Beyond Race and Borders

Everything I could See Was in Color
David Aspesi

Editors' Commentary

When most people think of segregation, they think of the archetypal Jim Crow-enforced schisms in American society. But discrimination occurs for reasons other than race, and outside the borders of the United States. Our ability to collect stories that took place outside of the United States was limited, but an increasing number of Central's freshmen were born in other countries or come from families with diverse beliefs and ethnic identities. The stories students have collected about international racism and discrimination based on something other than race from the children of immigrants and those with international experience was significant enough to warrant the creation of a category. These stories are all bonded by the common thread of discrimination. The people faced the same dehumanizing effects that blacks dealt with in the South. Their experiences were separated by context, but not content.

Sam Ivanovsky's essay presents the discrimination against the Jews in Russia taking on a similar level as the discrimination against Jews in Germany before Hitler's Final Solution took root. His essay also raises the question about how first-generation immigrants perceive opportunity in America as opposed to their children, who tend to take it for granted. Aya Kantorovich's essay was a fantastic piece with themes similar to that of Sam's. It had a gripping narrative and Aya clearly hadn't heard the story before. "Breaking a Barrier" offers a telling portrait of class relations in China several decades ago. The peasant farmers were oppressed and desperately poor. The essay has a very uplifting story, and shows how people can overcome discrimination individually. Siteng Ma's essay details changes in China that helped reverse situations like what was encountered in "Breaking a Barrier." Yeqian Xu's essay, "It's Not Just Race," deals with the Chinese government's suppression campaign against the Falun Gong religion. The propaganda, again, echoes the campaign against Jews by Nazi Germany and Stalin's Russia. Yeqian's story deals with the discrimination that occurred after the Cultural Revolution. The two essays about China work together to paint a portrait of civil rights growing and changing in a foreign country, and help show that the world today is the real battleground for civil rights, not just the South, not just long ago.

Hamza Arshad's essay, "Life After 911" has an interesting take on Americanization. After the police interrupted a party because a paranoid neighbor called in, assuming that a gathering of Muslims may just be a gathering of terrorists, his mother began dressing "like an American," and he put the pattern together. Kaitlyn Callahan's essay also dealt with American interactions with the Muslim world, and how 9/11 fostered a negative perception of Muslims that Michael Callahan had to overcome. Thomas Sanders' essay offers another unique take on the immigrant experience, like Hamza Arshad's. William Miranda escaped from the Nicaraguan military, and his experiences in the military shaped his opinions on immigration now. He offers a very poignant plea for aliens who have no other means of entry into the country. Finally, Jane Doe's essay, "I Almost Killed Myself," shows how mixed-race individuals encounter discrimination because of their race everywhere in the world. His plight wasn't much different than many children with black and white parents in the South.

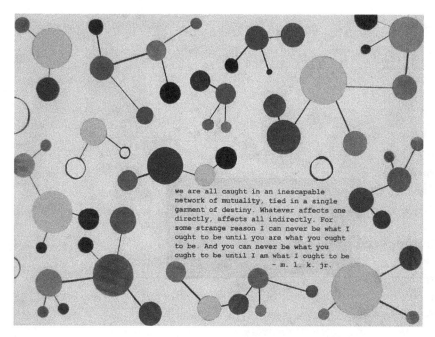

we are all caught in an inescapable
network of mutuality, tied in a single
garment of destiny. Whatever affects one
directly, affects all indirectly. For
some strange reason I can never be what I
ought to be until you are what you ought
to be. And you can never be what you
ought to be until I am what I ought to be
                                    ~ m. l. k. jr.

Network of Mutuality
Jennifer Perren

We Just Want to Live a Good Life, Too

When the news on the T.V. came on, we were in our living room. "Illegal immigration is hurting the U.S.," the voice said. My stepfather turned his head to pay attention. I watched his facial expressions on some of the topics. It really amazed me that, him being so tough and nothing ever bothering him, he was stricken by the comments. Later that night, I pondered on the thought, knowing that he was an immigrant but that he was legal. So why did it bother him? The next day is when I would sit down with William Miranda to hold a conversation.

Interviewer: Thomas Sanders
Interviewee: William Miranda
Time Period: 1990s
Location: United States
Affected Group: Hispanic
Setting: Public

When my stepfather walked through the door, it was just how I thought it would be: everything was a rush. He had just got back from work at 11:30 at night. I knew he was tired so I made it fast. The first question I asked him was, "How do you feel about the problem, as America would say, with the illegal immigrants?"

From that moment on he did not look tired at all. First he said, "Do you know what happened to me in Nicaragua?" I said, "No." Then he said, "We will start there first."

"I was born into a wealthy family in Nicaragua. My life was easy, I didn't even have to go to school, but I chose to so I could have an education. I was drafted into the army at 14, for the home government (the government that was already in power). We were fighting against the republicans who wanted to take over. I was sent on a suicide mission and was not expected to return. I was planning on running away, when boooom! We were under attack. I was shot in the back. And that is where my journey began. I faked my death. And when they bought it, I fled, wounded, toward the U.S.A." Mr. Miranda continued, "I was illegal when I arrived."

I asked, "What was going through your head?" He said, "Nothing, we, as most illegal immigrants, just want to live a good life too, are we at fault?" This stunned me, knowing that some illegal immigrants bring drugs.

"How do you feel about the illegal immigrants who bring drugs and chaos?" He replied, "I think they should all die." WOW! He is usually a soft and caring person. He then said, "They bring nothing but shame to our races and make it hard for the ones who try to make a good life, to get over here." Those comments stuck in my head forever, because I know him personally. "But don't you have illegal people working for you?" He replied, "Yes, but they are the ones who come over here to start a good life, and that's it."

"How does your family feel about you being over here?" was my next question. "They are jealous. Everyone in other countries is jealous of the U.S." "Why do think that is?" I asked. He replied, "Over here there is everything that can start a new good life, and America has so much meaning to the ones over here." I wondered why that was. He told me it was "Because now I can support my daughter and family, and I have a good job."

"Do you think it takes too long to become legal?" I asked him. "Yes, way too long. That is why everyone is getting in trouble. They can't get their cards, so they have to sneak around. And that makes them look guilty. If they could get them sooner, they would live a normal life. I mean, they do everything that you all [citizens] do, just in the shadows." Now I could tell I was sort of offending my stepfather so I decided to stop. I said, "Thank you." He didn't reply, which led me to assume that, although he is so tough on the inside, when it comes to illegal immigrants, he gets serious because he has been one himself.

Throughout the interview my stepfather was sad (and most of the time, mad). I have learned a lot from this, but also about him. Those are the questions and answers that have now changed two lives; and after more people read this, it will change their lives, too. So, next time you start to hate on illegal immigrants, put yourself in their shoes.

A Soldier's View of the People He Fought For and Against

I sat in my family's kitchen, armed with a note-book and brand-spankin'-new pen, ready and eager to conduct the interview. My dad, the subject of my dissection, was shuffling about the room, preparing the coffee-maker, doing the dishes, sweeping, and making detours to the pantry (all the while insisting, over the slam of pristine china, white cabinet doors, and a particularly painful American Idol contestant) that he could, in fact, answer questions while his hands were busy.

Michael A. Callahan's appearance wasn't exactly professional—comical might have been a better word. His incredibly mussed dark

Interviewer:
Kaitlyn Callahan

Interviewee:
Michael Callahan

Time Period:
2000s

Location:
Fallujah, Iraq

Affected Group:
Iraqi

Setting:
Public

brown hair, paired with the not-so-coordinating Little Rock Marathon t-shirt, Arkansas Razorback pajama pants, and fuzzy slip-pers, gave a somewhat different impression than the button down shirts, ties, slacks, shiny shoes, and Army uniforms that were the apparel he's most seen in. However, the kind, intelligent face was the same in any dress code, so most everyone sees him much the way I do as his daughter. Even that messy hair is a show of how he balances his work and home life with good humor—a relatively happy medi-um as far as length goes, somewhere between the buzz cut the Army likes, and the long by comparison hair my mother insists upon.

My dad's life was pretty quiet and unremarkable. He was born in Camden, Arkansas, and lived in California for a while as a child. When he was still young, his family, his parents, and one younger brother moved back to Arkansas, and much of his youth was spent roaming the hills and mountains of Danville, Arkansas, shotgun over one shoulder. He graduated along with a class of 42 people, some-thing that's made me shiver many a time. He then rode along to the

University of Arkansas at Fayetteville, which he left with a degree in Engineering and a bride. His father died of lung cancer in 2000, but his animated mother is well, thanks for asking, whether she thinks so or not. Now, at 40, he's a fantastic (and therefore busy) engineer and major in the United States Army Reserves, and is four years back from his tour in Iraq.

The focus of the careful interview of my father was his relations with Iraqis, and his views on the people that have such an effect on our country. Most of the discussion was turned to not so much stories as vague remembrances of people he worked with and people he met along the way.

Of all he said, what really resounded in my head after the interview was the two things he really learned during his deployment: the reality of the people of Iraqi and the wonder of home in America.

Captain Callahan, soon to be Major Callahan, was deployed to Fallujah, Iraq, as commander of the 489th Engineering Battalion. His battalion's job was to sniff out enemy weapons and dispose of them, sometimes in ways that would make the Mythbusters proud. Over the course of his duty, he also spent time in Kuwait, Bagdad, and Babylon, but the majority of his stay was in the not-so-sweet home of Fallujah. While there, he worked not just with other soldiers, but also with Iraqis.

When you spend large amounts of time with a group of people, particularly a group of people whose culture seems entirely other, you start to notice some things. One thing my dad noticed, because it caused a lot of problems for soldiers, is that they always say that they'll be somewhere or bring something or something will happen "tomorrow." Tomorrow, however, doesn't mean "the next day," it just means sometime in the future. Another thing that stood out was the Iraqi's etiquette at the table. All the food was served in a mountain on one or two plates, which people would share and eat off of with their hands, sticking said hands into their mouths during the process, much to the discomfort of the American guests. While neither of these seem like prime meat for a heart-warmer, one other thing that stood front and center was the gratitude that met him and his troops nearly everywhere they traveled. Many, many citizens thanked them for taking down Saddam Hussein, for bringing about something closer to peace and stability, for bringing a government for the people, and for delivering freedoms that had hitherto been unattainable. The women in particular, who previously had been below the feet of men in esteem and already limited rights, were ever thankful and ever fascinated by the female soldiers they met. In fact, these women warriors quickly became used to accented "I love yous" from them. Some of my favorite pictures from this year of my dad's life are those of children running to greet soldiers as they head down the dusty streets. There were other, smaller lessons that pointed toward America: from him, I learned that Twinkies taste like home, that families can grow closer as the distance between them grows greater, and home really is where the heart is.

From his experience with Iraqis, he really knew that he believed the war was worth a chapter of his life, a year of constant danger. He learned that these people are just that—people—human beings who should have the same "unalienable rights." The rights to "Life, Liberty, and the Pursuit of Happiness," rights that had been denied to them. Many differences lie between the Iraqi and American cultures, but there are just as many similarities: A want for betterment, frustration when that betterment is unreachable, desire to rule one's own life and government, the need to protect our families. All of the things that mark us as human, and the things that mark us as civilized, caring beings are shared. He also gained a stronger appreciation for America, for our freedoms and liberties, our equality, our way of life, our people-run government, and the family waiting for him at home.

I Almost Killed Myself

A glamorous office with high ceiling, shiny wooden floors, tons of piles of paperwork, and a comfortable black leather chair...this was the place where John Doe works. He is a tall, young looking Asian-American whose Russian and Chinese blood makes him so different. With an expensive suit and perfectly-polished black shoes, he looks so admirable. Women turn their heads when he walks by, and every child wishes to be fathered by him. But no one knows that under those smiles, he hides pains from a terrible period that would forever scar his brain.

Interviewer: Jane Doe
Interviewee: John Doe
Time Period: 1960s
Location: Russia
Affected Group: Chinese
Setting: Public

John was part of a unique family. His dad was Russian, and his mom was Chinese. Growing up in the capital of Russia, Moscow, life was hard for him. His dad did not earn much, and his mom was constantly sick. John had to start working to support his family's basic needs at a very young age. When he was 20, he moved to the United States to attend college, where he met his current wife, Jane Doe. After years and education and hard works, he is currently the head of the sales department at a well-respected company.

The interview conducted with John was an attempt to understand the emotional, physical, and psychological impacts of racism and stereotyping. The interviewee retold incidents during his childhood that showcased the reactions of others after seeing his family together- er. Furthermore, the interviewee expressed his feeling and his anger toward those incidents at that time. The progress made by people was mentioned during the interview. It showed how far people have come since then and how far the people of in this world still have to go. John described how those experiences changed him as a person in addition to the impact of those experiences.

One story that particularly stuck in my mind happened when Doe was only 6. John, his mom, and his dad were all at a grocery store doing their weekly grocery-shopping. When they were approaching the cash-register to check out, the cashier, who was an old Russian woman, gave him looks that were described as "disgusted and grossed-out." John, at that age, didn't know what they meant or why that happened. He smiled back at her, which made her even more "annoyed." When she was scanning the items, she started asking his parents what they were. Then she started yelling out names, such as "you traitor" at the dad. The tone of John's voice deepened as he described the words that she said to him, such as "you are such a bastard! I'm gonna kill you!"

This little incident impacted John greatly. He was so struck by this experience that he started resenting people. He would lock himself in his room and would not communicate with anyone fearing what people would say when they see his foreign face. Furthermore, those words made him question himself, and he wondered every night why people just wouldn't accept him. Tears filled his eyes as he said "I even came close killing myself..."

This story is related to the bigger history of America's struggle for "liberty and justice for all." Even though the incident didn't happened in the United States, it still showed that racism and stereotyping can have a great effect on children. John's experience demonstrated the way that minorities were treated. This proved that "liberty and justice for all" did not always happen no matter how people want to believe that it did. People were treated like trash, and it wasn't fair.

This interview really struck me. I didn't realize that history could have such a impact on a person's mental state. What surprised me the most was the fact that someone in my own family could have endured such pains. It changed my view on history of civil rights for the fact that the struggle for liberty did not only happened to the African-Americans in the U.S., but also to many other races and ethnic groups in other part of the world. I also realized that the struggle of civil rights has not ended. People are still fighting to completely eliminate prejudice. This can be shown through the fact that there has yet to be a woman or black president [as of this writing].

The Great Wheel of Law

My interviewee, Wu Tong, who is 69 years old, was an excellent source of knowledge and inspiration. Mrs. Wu is currently retired, but was previously occupied as an accountant in North Little Rock, Arkansas. She is the mother of my parents' friend. In her story, she demonstrated her courage and perseverance and has affected my personal view of her greatly.

A long time ago, Wu Tong and her husband lived in Handan, China. They were followers of a traditional Chinese self-cultivation practice called Falun Gong or Falun Dafa, which is similar to a fusion of Buddhism and Quigong. In Chinese, Falun Dafa translates as "the great wheel of law." Falun Dafa followers practiced their three golden rules of truthfulness, benevolence, and forbearance. The Chinese Communist Party, or CCP for short, viewed Falun Dafa as a threat to their strict, atheist teachings, since the popularity of the discipline was growing rapidly. In order to exterminate the threat of Falun Dafa, Zhang Zemin, the Chinese "president" at the time, outlawed the peaceful practice and suppressed it in any way possible. At first, the Communist Party spread propaganda in order to depict Falun Dafa practitioners as violent, malevolent, and a threat to the newly reformed, but unstable society. According to Mrs. Wu, the Chinese Communist Party would often send numerous "dangerous looking men in dark glasses" to the Falun Dafa events. Also, when the practitioners attempted to defend the discipline against the propaganda and change the clouded views of the people, the government immediately arrested thousands of Falun Dafa practitioners. The government even made anonymous threat calls to numerous followers of the discipline, including Wu Tong and her husband. Since the followers were arrested on the behalf of the Chinese Communist Party,

Interviewer:
Yeqian "Henry" Xu

Interviewee:
Wu Tong

Time Period:
1970s

Location:
Handan, China

Affected Group:
Falun Gong
followers

Setting:
Public

there were no trials or any chances of a fair argument. Thousands of followers had already been seized, imprisoned, and tortured in an inhuman way. Therefore, Mrs. Wu (now with a child) and her husband considered leaving China illegally to a safer place, though first they wanted to remain in their country and attempt to resist the Communists. Eventually, the anonymous calls from the government increased and in total fear and panic, Wu Tong and her husband Zhang Erkai left China in order to look for a safer place to live. Currently, the couple lives in North Little Rock and has lived there for approximately the last twenty years.

To me, Wu Tong's story has changed my perception of her from an average elderly Chinese woman to an extraordinary person with perseverance and courage. It was courageous indeed to attempt to resist the powerful, and at times, tyrannical Communist Party of China. Also, I was amazed by her ability to spend twenty years in the United States, which to her was a distant land with radically different language, culture, and people. Personally, Mrs. Wu's story has changed my view of many elderly people and taught me to respect them for their experiences and hardships. Most importantly, my eyes have been opened to the brutality, savagery, and mercilessness of my cruel people. Never before have I considered myself as a part of a nation that has committed genocide against its own people. Previously, I stubbornly believed that the Western, democratic countries exaggerated the numbers of Chinese men, women, and children killed by the government in order to make Communist China seem extremely tyrannical and Nazi-like. Though I am not to be moved from the fact that my nation is not as harsh as it seems, I am also certain that the numbers are certainly correct. Although my discovery angered and terrified me greatly, I am nonetheless proud of my roots, my ancestors, and my heritage. I also hope for a brighter and more liberating future for my country and that all the suffering did not have to do in vain, as well as a happier life for Mrs. Wu, an old, but courageous Chinese woman who had an exciting story to tell.

"When You Have No Choice, Mobilize the Spirit of Courage"
—Jewish Proverb

This is my interview with my parents:

Misha

Interviewer: Sam Ivanovsky
Interviewee: Misha and Marina Ivanovsky
Time Period: 1960s-1990s
Location: Russia
Affected Group: Jewish
Setting: School

Q: Can you give me your name?
A: I am Mikhail Ivanovsky

Q: What is your ethnicity?
A: I am a Russian Jew.

Q: What era did you mostly live in when you where in school?
A: I started school in 1972 and it was in Russia so it takes 10 years and it ended in 1982.

Q: During this time in Russia did you hear anything about the Central High Crisis?
A: In the Soviet Union they used all the things that were scandals and of high importance as propaganda. I bet that the Russians know more about African Americans in school though. Also many things that were bad with the Capitalist system.

Q: Mostly they were talking about America in general and not of a certain type of people such as African Americans?
A: They talked about the social system. They talked about how the government of America caused all these segregations and many negative things which were not true at all.

Q: **This was taught throughout all of your grades in school?**

A: Absolutely, they taught us that the Capitalist system is very bad. We haven't been exposed to these things so we thought it was true.

Q: **You're Jewish, and does your Jewish-ness give you a disadvantage?**

A: In Russia there are not many African Americans. Historically, the Jews did not have a home anywhere. Russia is very anti-Semitic. Many Jews went to the Revolution to eliminate the anti-Semitism but it didn't change a thing and still is an anti-Semitic country. There still exist many stereotypes. There was government anti-Semitism. At school they could not trace you by religion because the government was against religion and Judaism almost did not exist, so they didn't trace you by your beliefs. You were considered a freak if you were Jewish. They traced you by blood. If you were Jewish and looked Jewish then they knew. In Russia they put nationalities. Even in the class journal when they put the last name they put the nationality. They put Jew in front of your name. You just have to fight for your voice. I was considered a hooligan but my main thing was, and I was fighting for only one reason, and that was because of the Jewish slurs. During the school year, it was all the time. I had a friend who was a Jewish guy. He was semi-Jewish. He had a Jewish last name and then he changed his name to a Russian sounding one. He even changed it because he had legal rights. No one considered him Russian. I always went to him and asked, "Are you Russian or Jewish?"

Q: **Even in communist times did religion have a big impact on your social status?**

A: Because it's Communism, the official religion is Atheism. When I was in medical school, I was in Moscow. There was only one synagogue. I was told that every other person in this synagogue was a KGB agent. The other people were old people from the war. It was a pitiful thing. There were two official prayers, One for Communism and one for government. It was a joke.

Q: How did things change when you came to American?

A: America is a blessed country. Some American guys who were born in this country they don't fully appreciate the county. They don't understand the opportunities. In Russia they are going to trace you and you're going to be a Jew everywhere. In America, no one cares and you can convert and you can be who you want. Here you are not pushed toward maintaining your identity. I realize what the African Americans went through. Being Jewish and being a racist does not exist.

Q: Did you ever second question the propaganda?

A: The propaganda machine works very effectively. It was never direct. They show facts that are one sided. There is propaganda everywhere. Even here in America, you just have to have a clear mind. Stalin wanted to send all the Jews to Siberia to shield them from the righteousness from the good Russians. Because he thought the Jews wanted to destroy his power.

Q: Did being Jewish affect your career life, were you equal with everyone?

A: No, there was a quota. You have to be very good to compete with other people. Because the Jewish minority was small then they tried to not admit the Jews. The Jews knew about their discrimination. I wanted to get into a good Moscow medical school. My mom told me that it was almost impossible even with very high grades to get into it. I went to another school and passed with high honors. Then I switch to Moscow which was very difficult. No equal opportunities whatsoever.

Marina

Q: Your name?

A: Marina Ivanovsky

Q: Your ethnicity?

A: I am a Russian Jew.

Q: To start out with, in Russia were you equal with men?

A: Well I spent my life from 1972 to 1993 and only twenty one years. I did not think on my level as being a woman at that age. It's probably not true if you ask someone that's older.

Q: What was expected as a woman in Russia?

A: The Russian woman was supposed to take care of their family. Clean the house and prepare the meal and take care of the kids. The husband was the provider. There were no canned foods. You might have even had to grow the goods. A lot of people had problems during the women. There were no cars and woman had to walk to the stores and wait in lines. You had to buy a lot because you might not get another chance. In many cases there was 1 car for 20 families. ·

Q: Were the women encouraged to step up during the war?

A: Yes, in my family that left for World War II there was my grand-ma that was a tailor. She made coats. Her husband was on the battlefield while she was doing her work. Since the weather was very extreme she had to specialize in many different varieties and materials.

Q: How were the foreigners seen in the intuitions such as Arabs?

A: There were barely any of them. About 1-2 percent where foreign-ers. They studied in the Russian language but what they did have, they had dollars. A lot of students saw them as better because they had more money. If you ask them they probably had some occasions when they were beaten. It was very rare and people were not informed.

Q: How did you personally see Americans?

A: In school we were prepared for the Cold War. We were always reminded. We had to know the name of gases and taught how to use the AK-47. We had to do exercises with them. There was a mil-itary prep class also. I never dreamed of going to America. Someone who had relatives in America had an advantage of having their fancy items from America. Having a relative in America and living in Russia, you were looked upon as non-patriotic.

Q: Propaganda or personal beliefs had more of an impact of your view?
A: There were rebels against everything. I had a little of everything. The majority believed in propaganda. Since there was no freedom of speech or media, all of it was printed. There were also one or two channels that showed the same things. We had no other sources of other information. We were left to believe the one sided view of the world.

Being the son of these two independent people, I have a great responsibility upon my shoulders. I am the new generation of the family. As I heard all these stories about how many people were tricked or uninformed, I realized why we moved and the power of the country we live in right now. Rising above all of these negative influences, both my parents strived for success and reached the top. I always look back and ask my dad, "What if we stayed?" This is when he tells me that the best decision of his life was to move here and that we should use this opportunity for the greatest.

I have always known that my parents were achievers and believers, but I didn't realize how much their appearance or name had such a big impact. You would not think that how you look affects your career, but for them, it did also succeed with disadvantages and people against you is another great feat. I always know that I need to be pushed just as hard to get as much as they did. So I understand now why parents care so much.

Some people look at me as a product of my parents' success. I was the product of America and not my parents. People are blind from what struggles you have to go through to achieve the top. They look and assume that I am a rich kid that just gets everything so easily. Just at the tips of my fingers. Oh, it's not that way at all. They are blind from what they have here. What's stopping them except their own ignorance? When my family came to America, we were on welfare living in horrible conditions. Welfare and food stamps is what we survived on. I was a child and needing much attention at that time. It was hard to survive but Dad and Mom stuck to the end and achieved what we have now. This shows that anything is possible if you just realize what you have. We rose and rose and now we can look back and say what a great trip it was because it was worth every single struggle and pain.

The Runaway Escape

There are many things that I learned and saw during my grandmother's interview. One thing I saw was the computer, with its light screen glare and then the sudden sight of my grandma. The blonde hair and large glasses that covered her face were the most obvious detail about her. That and followed be a raspy "hello" and slight coughs mixed with Russian language.

Interviewer:
Aya Kantorovich

Interviewee:
Lera Luria

Time Period:
1940s

Location:
Lydia, West Belarus

Affected Group:
Jewish

Setting:
Neighborhood

My dad was in the other room. He constantly came to check on the computer and comment on my grandmother's improvement in Hebrew.

The bright light first filled my eyes and took a while to get accustomed to. Her short hair and large gray sweater seemed to combine. Lera, my grandma, with her aged skin that wrinkled slightly and her Russian wisdom means the world to me.

A teacher, that's what she was, a Physics one, to be precise. She was born in Lydia, Belarus, and her father and mother were both factory workers. She married and lived in Lithuania and finally moved to Israel as her final destination. The purpose of this interview was to understand what my grandma, and other people living in that time frame, had to face. Many of the things that we talked about were the things she heard from either her mother or father, and many of her thoughts afterward.

This is her history, her story, occurring when she was from half a year till she was a little over four. This is my family's history, only she is the one to tell it to me now. It occurred during World War II when the Holocaust began and she ran with her mother and father to get to safety and away from the Nazis.

My grandma was quite young then. She wishes she had asked her mother all the questions that had built up inside of her. Only she didn't get a chance; her mother died shortly after the war ended, quite young.

As I said before, she was born in Lydia, in western Belarus. Even at that time, Belarus belonged to Russia—the Soviet Union. When World War II occurred, it didn't take long to start hunting the Jews, and that's when her and her parents fled to the woods, with the help of some partisans.

Her story began when the war starts and their town is going to get burned and hit by bombs. My grandmothers' father, being a partisan and a known factory worker, started the evacuation and helped almost everyone escape the town with any transportation they had. Once there were no more cars left, my family, and others who were also left, escaped the town by foot, and fled to the woods. They found a house with people willing to help, and as my grandmothers' dad worked, these kind people gave them food and shelter. Both my grandmothers' parents gave food and medicine to the partisans, even though they had little for themselves. The medicines came from a German doctor, who knew my grandmothers' dad had contact with the partisans, so he gave them the medicines that they needed. My great-grandmother kept the medicines and food in a blanket that she would carry with her, and conceal what was inside, and sent it to the partisans.

At age three, someone told on my family, saying that they were Jews, and they got put in jail. My great-grandfather was sent by an inspector to a doctor to see if he was circumcised in order to tell if he was Jewish. It turns out that the doctor was the old German doctor that knew my family and gave them medicines to the partisans. The doctor lied and told the inspectors that he wasn't Jewish and they were mistaken. Later, after the war, the same doctor traveled to America where he was put in jail for being accused of helping the Germans. My great-grandfather went to the judges and told them how much that doctor had helped my family, and he was set free.

My grandmother felt many things. She was scared and frightened, but also confused because she did not know what was going on and she was so young. She says that "the older I get, the more I start to remember certain memories." One of the things that occurred during the interview that really sticks in my mind until now is that quote, when she tells of how she starts to remember, and how she wished she could ask her mother the many unanswered questions that she has.

Since the war, although she was young, my grandmother takes more caution knowing that they could have been a rich situated family if the war had not begun. She minds the decisions that she makes by thinking about the past. Her career was a choice she wanted to take, to teach people something that she knows best. My grandma's history impacts her, making her want to teach younger people more than what they already know.

I think that this interview sticks in my mind because it was a time when one particular religion was picked on by millions. The fact that I am also Jewish and that this is my history contributes to the fact that I care and understand how my family and my people had to struggle because people didn't like Jewish people. The amount of things that my family has lost makes me so upset that my family, unlike some other families, had to lose so much because of their religion. One thing that really surprised me was the will of the German doctor to help those in need even though he knew the consequence could be death.

This is important because this is the history when over six million Jewish people were massacred! This doesn't happen on a daily basis, and the fact that only one religion was picked on this way is very unfair and unjust. No other religion has ever lost this many people over the course of four years, and on purpose. We need to remember so that history will never repeat itself and let this tragic thing happen all over again.

In the future, anyone who is doing this Memory Project should know that in order to really be able to relate and understand the interviewee, the interviewer must put themselves in their shoes and try to picture if they could outlive something that great and harsh. Only when the interviewer does that, then the reader realizes that they can picture and relate to the interviewee just so and learn from their experiences.

Life After 9/11

On the stove was something being cooked in a pot. Around the stove, ingredients littered the surroundings. The sink was empty, all the dishes sitting out to dry. I sat in a chair around the dining table noticing all this just before my interview. My mother was cooking some curry, a Pakistani dish that requires one to slowly cook ingredients in a pot for 20-30 minutes for dinner. As my mom sat down in the chair beside me, I had many questions for her, but as my interview progressed, they were all answered.

My mother was born in Lahore, Pakistan. She lived there for many years. She also lived in Bahrain because of her father's job. Later she moved back to Pakistan and got married. Shortly after being married, she moved to America. First she lived in San Francisco, California, then Los Angeles, California, and then finally in Little Rock, Arkansas. My mother is a house wife who spends her time with us, her kids.

Interviewer:
Hamza Arshad

Interviewee:
Lubna Arshad

Time Period:
2000s

Location:
Little Rock, AR

Affected Group:
Muslims

Setting:
Neighborhood/
Public

The story that stuck the most in my mind was that of the 9/11 attack. My mom told me that before then, nobody thought of us in any sort of negative manner, but ever since the attack, people thought and acted differently toward us. We were never directly talked about, but there was a lot of indirect stuff affecting us.

After 9/11, we were supposed to go to a birthday party at one of my mother's friend's house. When we got to the person's house, we sat there and talked for some time and then later ate some cake. It was then that for some reason the police came. I was told by my mom later "that the neighbors called and informed the police of suspicious activity being done at the house, since there were so many Asian-looking people going into a single house." At this party, about twenty families were invited and all of us were wearing traditional Pakistani clothing.

This experience changed my mother in more ways than one. After this incident, I noticed that my mom started wearing less traditional clothing and more jeans and shirts. Before this incident involving the police, my mother barely wore American clothing, but after this incident she barely wore traditional Pakistani clothing outside of our house. Another change I noticed with my mother was that before the incident, she would drive around by herself doing the daily tasks, but after the incident, she always takes somebody with her to do errands.

My mom's story can easily relate to the bigger story of America's struggle for "liberty and justice for all." This story relates to the discrimination and stereotyping of religion and race. My family was discriminated against because of our religion, since we are Muslim. The bigger story of America's struggle for "liberty and justice for all" ties into racial prejudice; in each time period, one group or another have been stereotyped because they looked like or were from a specific group or background. Until we take down these barriers, I believe we will not reach our goal of "liberty and justice for all."

I believe this interview has changed me in more ways than one. It has changed me in the way I look at society. Now when I look at society, I see many racial and religious barriers which have been set up by the people in society to blame their own problems. This interview has also given me a sense of pride, that even after being through so much, my parents have never done anything derogatory toward the people who have treated us so. A tip for people doing an interview is that you only need to ask one or two questions, because after those questions have been asked, memory begins to spill out of the person's mind; all you have to do is record it.

Breaking a Barrier

My father was born in 1964 in a very rural part of southeastern China. He was accepted into Stanford University at age 34. He received his Ph.D. in medical physics at age 38. Currently, at 41 years of age, he resides in Little Rock, Arkansas, with his wife and two children and is working at the University of Arkansas of Medical Sciences as a medical oncologist.

Interviewer:	Jane Doe
Interviewee:	John Doe
Time Period:	1980s
Location:	China
Affected Group:	Chinese
Setting:	Public

To understand the challenges that my father went through, one must understand that China's culture and way of life are very different compared to American life. The rich people were incredibly rich and the farmers had nothing. The people who were educated lived in the city and looked down upon farmers, which made up about 90% of the population. The farmers were discriminated against because they were uneducated and poor. To have an idea of how poor the farmers were, my father told me a story about a boy in his village. This boy's family was just as poor as the rest of the people in the village. He had a horrible fever and the doctor couldn't do anything. As a dying wish, he wanted to have a bowl of white rice because his family could not afford it all his life. The family went around the village asking for rice and made him a bowl to eat. In the end, his fever broke and he survived. With an impression on how my father grew up, I will tell his story.

My father was born in 1964. He was the second oldest of four children. He has a big sister and two little brothers. When my father was little, he worked night and day in the fields. When he had the time, he would go to the only teacher in the village and learned to read, write, and do math. His father discouraged learning because work was overwhelming and there wasn't time. My father kept on going to the teacher. He was a thinker; he made a promise to himself at an early age that he would not grow up as a farmer. Nobody in his

entire village had ever gone to college. His father strongly discouraged him from doing that because they didn't have the money to send
him to college. The chances of my father making it all the way
through school were very small because of the discrimination against
farmers. When his father told him that he could not leave the village
to go to college, my father ran away at the age of 15 with nothing but
his life savings and the clothes on his back.

He traveled to the city and attended a school to get his diploma.
To pay for tuition, he worked as a janitor and washed dishes. He
knew that his chances were small, so he gave everything that he had
to pursue his dream. He saved some money and bought a violin. On
weekends, he would practice for the entire day in an abandoned
classroom. He was very interested in music and learned how to play
the violin, harmonica, guitar, and bass guitar in a few years. He got
accepted into an aeronautics college and he was working on becoming an airplane engineer at age 19. To pay for college, my father
could not earn his tuition all by himself so he contacted home for
help. His sister, who cared about him very much, gave him her wedding dowry to help him finish college. He started working when he
was 25 and that was when he first met my mother. They got married
in a year. After three years of working as an engineer, my father was
unsatisfied with his low salary and wanted to be something better. He
decided to go back to college and get a degree in physics. He stayed
in college for six more years to get a Master's in Medical Physics. By
the time he graduated, I was already seven years old. He was the best
student in his class so his school sent him to Stanford University in
California to get a Ph.D. My father took my mom and me to a little
town called Palo Alto. I spent the rest of my childhood there while
my father was working hard to attain a Ph.D. After getting his degree
at 36, he was offered a job as a medical oncologist at the University
of Arkansas for Medical Sciences. For those not familiar with the
term, he operates and designs the radiation machines that are used to
treat cancer patients. So we moved to Little Rock and have been living here since then. Now, he is a very respected member of the
National Society of Physicists. Every year, we send back enough
money so that my dad's entire family could be living life comfortably

like we are. China has improved since then. Many people from my dad's village followed his footsteps. He is proud to say that he took part in breaking down the barrier that kept the farmers in China from ever getting an education.

We could have moved back to China many years ago where he would be paid much more by the government. I asked him why we didn't move back and he said, "In China, your opportunities are limited; I wanted you to have as big of a future as you would like so that's why we stayed." After hearing my dad's story, I decided that I was so incredibly lucky to have such an overachiever as a father to motivate me in everything that I do.

People Began to Look at Each Other as Individuals, Rather Than Which ID You Held

The room was dark and quiet with a light in the corner, dim enough to portray the sense of a warm and pleasant home. A king sized bed was surrounded by walls with various drawings from my younger brother and a small painting on the wall directly behind it. My mom, sitting comfortably on it, began to speak. She was dressed in house clothes and long black hair embraced her head with brown eyes and a distinct smile. Thus, she began to speak.

Interviewer: Siteng Ma
Interviewee: Cuiwu Ma
Time Period: 1980s
Location: China
Affected Group: Chinese
Setting: Neighborhood/ Public

My mom, Cuiwu Ma, was born during the Cultural Revolution, a time of change and movement from the old ways to a more modern China. When she was 14, she lived in historic Kaifeng, Henan, a fairly large city in central China. It was the early 1980s. As a high school student, she barely knew what was going on in China's quickly-reforming political society.

Mao Zedong, the first Chairman of the Chinese Communist Party, established a series of government issued jobs, housing, regulated places to live and ID cards in an attempt to make the common Chinese citizen more productive. People living on a farm could not move to or even visit a city or town without permission from the government. IDs denoted the town which you were supposed to reside and work in. It was difficult or impossible to work or even live in another place, especially if you were a farmer trying to move into any city. The policies created by Chairman Mao belittled his very own supporters, the rural farmers and countrymen. That was back in the 1950s. When my mom was in high school, the creator of the Open

Door Policy, Deng Xiaoping, reformed Chairman Mao's system in a series of "Strategies to Promote Economic Development." Chairman Mao's policies were lightened, and it was possible to move from town to town and even get a job, but it involved heavy discrimination and often a very hefty fee paid to the government.

My mom went to school in a large intercity school during the migration of rural people into the cities for better job and living opportunities in the 1980s. She mentions the steadily increasing amount of farmers' children that went to her school over her four years of high school. The farmers' children were often very poor and even had to pay tuition to the intercity school simply because they were from out of the city and were often called ugly names because of their different ways of speaking, dressing, and acting. Although my mom was never quite aware of this influx, she began to make many friends with these people, even though they held a different ID and were different from the intercity kids. Gradually, with the increased population from farming communities coming into the intercity high school, discrimination lessened.

When a person or group of people from an unfamiliar culture or background comes in to the "mainstream society," often they are regarded as lesser beings and individuals. However, they too are human beings and ascend into "mainstream society" with increased population and influence. My mom, though not directly affected by the influx of farmers into the city during the 1980s, learned to make friends with these people and to regard them "as individuals, rather than what ID they held." She eventually became more interested in the things going on in the government and became more aware of Chinese politics and current events, and fully supports the set of reforms begun by Deng Xiaoping. Even though life in China is much easier and more equal today, the system is still reforming. My mom believes that China needs to get rid of the ID cards, which are still issued today.

Not only do civil rights struggles like the ones in China occur frequently, but also similar ones exist in the United States. The farmers and residents of rural China were fighting for a better education, job, and working place, but this has occurred in America as well ever since the founding of the USA. Although the struggle between people of different racial ethnicity has all but ended in America, struggles between the lower and upper class in China still exist to this day. Perhaps China should learn from America's example: "With liberty and justice for all," regardless of race, gender, class, or any other sort of characteristics.

It's Not Just Race

On November 28, 2004, I interviewed my dad, John Doe, about some violated civil rights in China in the late 1970s. One situation took place almost right after the Cultural Revolution and my dad was still in high school, ready for college. The Cultural Revolution in China was a period in time where communism was especially strong. It was formed by communist leader Mao Zedong. The government closed all colleges and people were gradually becoming more uneducated. Mao Zedong also encouraged the Red Guard (young people faithful to Mao's regime) to attack traditional values. The Cultural Revolution resulted in deaths of many intellectuals and independent thinkers and threw the country into total anarchy. With the death of Mao Zedong in 1976, the Cultural Revolution ended.

Interviewer:
Jane Doe

Interviewee:
John Doe

Time Period:
1970s

Location:
China

Affected Group:
Chinese

Setting:
School

As my dad was thinking about his future in his sophomore and junior year in high school, the colleges started opening again. Most students during the Cultural Revolution settled with the minimum education the government provided. However, as college qualifying exams opened up, students who had worked harder were rewarded. My dad and one of his best friends studied harder than ever because they knew they had to be the best, or at least one of the best, to get out of the poor conditions they had to endure. Throughout the year, they both went to many competitions to improve their record. My dad excelled in physics while his friend excelled in math. But there was one big difference between my dad and his friend: his friend had a handicap. As they both applied to take the college qualifying exam, the friend was informed that he was not able to even try it because he was handicapped. The friend was furious but no one could do anything. My dad took the test and was able to go to the best college in China. After some years in Beijing University, my dad took another test and was rewarded with a scholarship to leave China and go to the US, while his friend never had a chance for higher education and was forced to settle with a job in the local workshop.

My dad recently went back to China expecting a big change in the way citizens were treated. Shanghai had changed a lot but as he walked into a fast food restaurant, (part of a large chain) he saw a "HELP WANTED" poster. It was advertising a job as a janitor in that restaurant. The requirements were very strict and included an age limit: 20 to 30. If a 40 year old man can't even work as a janitor at a fast food restaurant, what other so-called rules are legal? This story is important because it shows that you didn't only have to be a different color, race, or religion to be discriminated against. Stereotypes are often formed on things like physical fitness, social status, appearance (weight/attractiveness), etc. Also discrimination doesn't only go on in America; it exists all over the world wherever there are living things.

America is actually pretty much discrimination-free when you compare it to nations like Israel, where the Israelis and Palestinians have fought civil wars for years and people on the street attack each other because of their nationality. This interview showed me how ridiculous some governments are to try to control their people. It's frustrating to try to look into the minds of these people.

Chapter Five:
Toward Acceptance

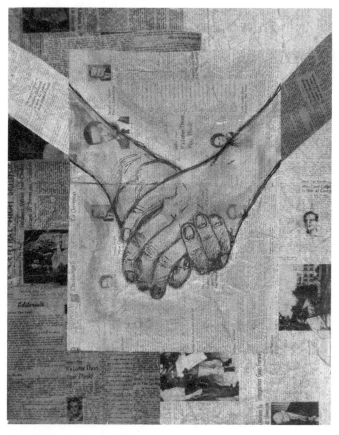

Untitled (mixed media) [hands clasped]
Allie Thompson

Editors' Commentary

Activism is a broad societal phenomenon. It's the winds of change blowing. Those protesting and demonstrating for change frequently meet with formidable obstacles: they have to combat entrenched opponents, the state, or popular opinion. Essays about demonstrators and activists comprised a significant portion of essays we reviewed. Those who combated segregation and discrimination often had powerful narratives, and they merited inclusion. In several of these essays, the student author as well as the interviewee chose to be identified simply as John Doe, often out of a fear of reprisal or some negative consequence.

When reading the essays in this section, it is important to remember that heroes on the home front are just as valuable as the soldiers on the news. Like the story of the Little Rock Nine, there are many incidents that the media picked up and that everyone now knows about. However, there are millions of activists who changed the course of history in small towns or neighborhoods, but who were never recognized by the world. Robert Sells was one of those undocumented heroes. He gave a man the self confidence to walk into a job interview with only white people. While that didn't cause mass uproar or social chaos, it did change the direction of Lee Roy Grant's future. In Jonathan Carraway's essay, the grocery owner had to face a mob because he helped a black family with their groceries. Being the better person and standing up for someone else's rights, like the way Jerry Meeks protected the people in his school, was quite a feat. Some people worked quietly to end the racism, like Dr. William Weaver who removed the "white" and "black" signs from his waiting room bathrooms. Daniel McGough tried to help the minorities who were being wronged in his area by voting to make housing discrimination illegal and also by supporting the United Farm Worker's Union in California to help the mostly Mexican workers. The support on the small scale made the impacts of the huge demonstrations even more important and understandable.

"Lost Hope" is an essay that involves a widely publicized event: the Tiananmen Square protest. The essay has an excellent narrative, and the old wounds are still present in the interviewee. The same sort of scarring apparent in "Lost Hope" is there in Hannah Baroni's essay, showing how damaging the adversity that activists face can be. Jennifer Perren's essay had that same quality as well: Earline Prince's flashback about the dogs at the Children's March disturbed her greatly. In Hannah Baroni's, Phillip Baroni is still haunted by the Klansmen who attacked him. A rare viewpoint is shown from the reflections of a news reporter for the *New York Times* in Selma in Vincent Reed's interview of Roy Reed. His explanation of the incident landed on the front page of the news paper and led to even greater actions during the Civil Rights Movement.

Almost all of the activists have suffered some injury for their attempts at making the world a better place. Success is a lot less likely than failure. Their motivations vary. Mostly, they were young people wanting to better their world. "Lost Hope" features a student who wanted his government to function properly. Joseph Berleant's had a woman from Buffalo who wanted her nation to be more tolerant toward other races. Activism can be fueled by a deep patriotism or a love of a certain group of people, and these essays all have people compelled to action to better their world on whatever scale.

Reflection of Hope
Samuel Weekley

We Wanted to Show the Whole Country That We Thought Segregation Was Ridiculous

My name is Joseph Berleant. I go to Central High in the class of 2012. I am in Mr. Johnson's Civics class and decided to interview my great-aunt, Helene Ageloff, a Freedom Rider during the 1950s and 1960s.

I interviewed Helene Ageloff over the telephone. She is my grandmother's sister and is retired. Her husband is Lawrence Ageloff, and they live in Maryland.

My great-aunt was very eager to describe her experience as a Freedom Rider. It was not hard for her to tell me about the events leading up to her involvement and the events that occurred during the Freedom Ride she was on.

Interviewer: Joseph Berleant
Interviewee: Helene Ageloff
Time Period: 1950s-1960s
Location: Mississippi
Affected Group: African American
Setting: Public

"Around 1956, there was movement toward equal education. At that time, the 'separate but equal' doctrine was still in effect. I was involved with that movement even though it was really hard to do. I was living in Buffalo, NY when we started. I helped to organize a demonstration for desegregation. I moved to Washington in 1960 and that was when I got involved in the Freedom Rides.

"The Rides led to efforts to increase African American voting registration. Even though change didn't happen quickly because people didn't want to give up power, the change slowly happened. There were many power struggles. It culminated with the march on Washington, D.C. when Martin Luther King, Jr. was jailed for his involvement.

"Lots of support for this change came from African American churches who helped in peaceful ways.

"I participated in a Freedom Ride in Jackson, Mississippi. A group of students, including me, went from New Orleans to Jackson on a train. We were the second group to come down here, and we wanted to show the whole country how much we wanted to change the situation.

"In Jackson, we had lunch and drank from a white water fountain. Even though some of us were white, we were all arrested because some of us were African American. The charge against us was for 'disturbing the peace.' We went to jail and then were put before a judge, who sentenced us to stay in jail.

"We were put in the Jackson city jails. The men were separated from the women and the African Americans form the whites. The cells were about 20 feet by 20 feet. Our aim was to fill up the jail with people after people. The cell I was in became very crowded. The cell next to ours had African Americans.

"It was several weeks before we were brought again before a judge, and we were sentenced to jail again. We could ask for a bail, but we chose to stay in the jail to help fill the cells. Then a huge group of people came from all over the country, so we were sent to a Mississippi penitentiary.

"This was a more serious jailing place. In the penitentiary, there were only two to three people per cell. We were getting lots of publicity, but we were still being mistreated very badly. Although no actual harm was inflicted upon us, we were given bad food and conditions in general were not nice. The people here tried to make us as uncomfortable as possible without actually hurting us. After that, we had a lawyer's group representing us.

"But the scariest part happened when we were discharged from the penitentiary. We asked to put a bail for us to come back for the hearing rather than stay there. A few people, depending on when they had come, were released. A few people were released at a time. I was released with some other people, and we were released in a car. The car wasn't driven directly back to the police headquarters like it was supposed to. The drivers took us in a roundabout way. There were like thugs. They took us to someplace else, where we weren't supposed to go. Luckily, the people at this wrong place decided to take us back to the right place."

Throughout the interview, I learned a lot about both the history of the Freedom Rides, their effects, and my great-aunt. I had not had a lot of contact with her, so the fact that she was a participant in the Freedom Rides was both interesting and enlightening. Also, I had not done much research on the Freedom Rides, so I learned a lot about how they came about, and how they helped to increase the rights of African Americans. I really look at my great-aunt differently now that I know that she was very involved in the Civil Rights Movement for African Americans. I'm glad I had this interview, not only because it taught me a lot about my great-aunt, but also because I learned a lot about the Freedom Rides, their causes, and how they affected the rights of African Americans.

Civil Rights in Mississippi

"I remember car bombings, cross burnings, and having my family's house shot at during a riot in 1967." These are the words of Philip Baroni when asked to remember what he went through during the fight for civil rights in the mid-1960s. Philip is about 54 years old. He has brown hair and blue-ish green eyes. His teen years were interrupted by fighting, riots, and fear. You could feel the atmosphere of the vividly decorated living room change when the topic was brought up. The warm, cheerful mood changed to solemn and dark. I noticed the dark gray color of the walls as Philip began to tell his story.

Interviewer: Hannah Baroni
Interviewee: Philip Baroni
Time Period: 1960s
Location: Mississippi
Affected Group: Caucasian
Setting: Home

Growing up in Natchez, Mississippi, in a white middle class family during the Civil Rights Movement taught him a lot about life. Philip's mother was very involved in the civil rights movement in Natchez. From the ages of 13 to 15 is when the events of the Civil Rights Movement most affected Philip. Philip attended Catholic schools which were not integrated at all. He recalls that during one of his years in high school, there was only one black child in his class. Now, 30 years later, Philip continues to live in the South. Today he works as the Outpatient Administrator at UAMS.

Philip was a very deserving candidate for this interview. Finding out about his past was very worthwhile and gave me a new outlook on what he and his family went through. He talked about a wide variety of subjects dealing with the peak of the civil rights movement in Natchez during the 1960s. The main person talked about in this interview is Philip's mother. She was most involved in the movement and was most affected. Unfortunately, she could not be interviewed because she passed away many years prior to the interview. Philip recalls many things about racial discrimination that he witnessed in the interview. He also speaks about what price his family had to pay to help others gain rights.

One story that seemed to have made an impression on him was the murder of Medgar Evers and several other NAACP officials during 1964. Charles Evers, Medgar's brother, was the leader of the civil rights movement in Mississippi during the 1960s. Philip's mother worked very closely with Mr. Evers during the course of the Civil Rights Movement. This story was probably important to Philip because he realized the injustice of this occurrence. Another very vivid memory Philip has was of a riot in 1967. During this riot, his house was shot at and he witnessed cross burnings, probably by the Ku Klux Klan. He also remembers his father having to check every morning for a bomb in his car because of the threats his family received. These memories seem very vivid and have stuck with Philip all of his life.

Philip's past has definitely made an impact on him. Though there is no way for me to directly compare the way he was as a child, or just after the events occurred, to the way he is now, you can tell that there is no way he is the same. A person can not endure these events and come out the same as when they began them. Today, Philip is not racist at all because he understands the importance of civil rights for everyone. He has a definite dislike for people who are close-minded about racial issues.

The story is just an atom on the grand scales of stories about civil rights. Philip went through and witnessed sheer hatred toward his family merely because his family wanted justice. This small story relates to what America went through during the fight for civil rights. I'm sure that there are tons of stories out there similar to this one. This story simply shows what one American family went through during the civil rights movement.

This story has had a significantly important impact on me. I learned what it was like to live in times when fear was everywhere. Hearing about civil rights makes me realize how lucky we are today.

The City Was Ablaze With the Fires of Hatred

The person that I interviewed was not only one person, but rather two people. These two people were Donna and Jerry Meeks, my grandparents. They are both retired teachers who have worked hard all of their lives to make this world a better place. Unfortunately, I was not able to interview them in person because the holidays took us apart from each other. So I interviewed them over the phone on Wednesday, November 22, 2006. I chose to interview them because I could think of no other people that could quite tell the stories that they had to tell about the Civil Rights Movement. They both worked in school districts in Memphis, Tennessee, and the Arkansas Delta for a time while the movements were going on. They had witnessed a lot over those years and I knew that no one could explain the rights movements or have more motivating experiences quite like these two.

Interviewer:
Shelby Held

Interviewee:
Jerry Meeks

Time Period:
1970s

Location:
Tennessee

Affected Group:
African American

Setting:
School

My grandparents' daughter, my mother, was in the second grade and having a birthday party in 1970. She asked if she could invite a few black girls to her party. They let her invite them, but when she asked this they were shocked. It was unheard of to invite blacks over. But these were the times that my grandparents grew up in; these were the customs that they were used to. They grew up in a time when racism was okay. They were brought up in a society that taught them to look down on others who were not like them, like the African Americans. They were taught that whites were superior to everyone else and nothing could change that. Everyone had black maids and servants and the blacks did not have any jobs higher than that. The blacks had to sit at the back of buses and could not even think about sitting in front. In movie theaters, they were forced to sit on the top

balcony, barely able to see the movie that was playing. They had separate bathrooms, separate drinking fountains, and separate everything until things started to change. These changes were known as
the Civil Rights Movement. My grandparents began to witness
changes where they lived. The African Americans no longer had separate facilities or seats at the back of the bus or top-balcony movie
seats. They could now sit where they wanted and they started to integrate schools, like elementary schools. They were finally becoming
people instead of just pieces of trash. They were finally becoming
individuals with rights.

   Along with these rights came trouble and conflicts between people. My grandparents were living in Memphis, Tennessee, at the time.
They were hearing on the news that troops were being used to integrate Central High School. "I was afraid that this same thing was
going to happen in Memphis, that these soldiers would be sent here
and fight," my grandmother told me. Martin Luther King, a civil
rights leader, was in town in Memphis when he was shot and killed.
He was there for a garbage worker strike that was going on throughout the town. After King's death, the garbage workers began to burn
things throughout the city and the whole town became lit up with fire
as fear and madness began to erupt. My grandmother was in the hospital at the time on the fourteenth floor and remembers seeing flames
and things burning all around the town. Three or four blocks down
from where my grandparents lived was a National Guard camp. At
that time, my grandfather was an assistant principal at a school in
Memphis. He often times needed to call a substitute teacher when a
teacher called in sick and their place could not be filled. At the school,
there were many black teachers and they started calling and saying
they could not attend school because they were being threatened that
their house would burn down or they would be shot if they even just
came to school. My grandfather began to receive bomb threats every
day because of the blacks that were in the school. As a result, two or
three police cars were sent to campus every day to make sure that
nobody got into the school without a legitimate reason to be there.

   But all of these changes have made my grandparents better people. Back in those times, they resented and were afraid of what was

going on. My grandparents were fearful of the African Americans of that time, afraid of their attitudes and afraid that the African Americans would hurt them. In other words, they were hard-core racists. They didn't care what happened to the blacks, as long as they did not have equal rights that the white people of the day enjoyed. But, over the years, as my grandparents have seen the hardships that African Americans had to go through and how really tough they had it, their opinions have changed. They now have much more tolerance and respect for people who are not like them. They believe that they should have equal rights. My grandparents have also pursued careers that made them try to better society and help people get along better together, which is one of the reasons that my grandfather became a minister. These events forced people to do one of two things: "be more tolerant of others or become much more prejudiced than they already were," my grandfather said.

Although much has changed and things have become better, my grandparents still do not believe that the road to integration is fully complete. My grandfather said, "The purpose of integration was to raise blacks to the same level whites had and I don't think that that has happened." He also believes that another purpose of integration was for blacks to adapt and adopt some of our white culture and become a part of it, but he believes that whites have picked up more black culture than blacks have picked up white culture. An example of this was when he was teaching civics one year, many years ago. They were studying about the unions. He then asked the question "How do you bring about reform?" One black student answered his question; he told him to "beat up or burn down." This very idea is the mindset of many people today in life, to beat it up or burn it down. My grandparents still believe that there is much work to be done in order for the Civil Rights Movement to be fully completed, but we are getting there one step at a time.

During this interview, I learned many things. I did not know about the harsh times that were prevalent at that time, and I did not know how hard life really was back then. I knew that there were separate facilities and things like that, but during this interview, these facts were shown to me that life really was that way back then. They were brought out to me in such a way that they were made real to me and not just a fact that you hear about on the news or you see in the paper. That was what everyone back then had to go through, including my grandparents, which made me see the past and my grandparents in a different light. I had not previously known that they were people who favored racism, but that's the way everyone was back then and they did not know any better. Because of this they are now trying to make up for their past. They are now making the world a better place for the people that they had once shown hatred and abhorrence toward. Even though the journey of racism and equalization is not yet over, it is becoming one step closer to doing so, slowly but surely.

The Fear Still Existed

Four hundred and eighty two years after Queen Isabella of Spain declared that all indigenous peoples in the lands Columbus had discovered were to be considered her subjects. Three hundred and twelve years after Anthony Johnson became the first free black man in North America. Eighty four years after the Jim Crow Laws were put into effect, and 17 years after the Central High Crisis. Four hundred and eighty two years is a long time, but what about 17? Most people would say that that is a long enough time period for conflicts between people to blow over. For Lee Roy Grant, an African American, fear still remained inside of him. For Robert Sells, he was trying to show African Americans that we are all equal.

Interviewer:
Anna-Lee Pittman

Interviewee:
Robert Sells

Time Period:
1970s

Location:
Little Rock, AR

Affected Group:
African American

Setting:
Restaurant

Robert Kenneth Sells, better known as Bob, was a Caucasian born and raised in Kansas City, Missouri. He was born on October 29, 1932 and is now currently retired. He attended the University of Missouri in Colombia and graduated from the "J" (journalism) School. At the time of this event, he was head of the Southwestern Bell Public Relations Department. One day he got a call from a friend telling him that he should interview this man for an opening position at the agency. Bob agreed. The man said the only problem was that he was an African American. Bob didn't care and told him to send him for an interview. The African American went by the name of Lee Roy Grant. He lived in Little Rock, Arkansas, and his parents were from there also. He attended Arkansas State University in Jonesboro, Arkansas. He was the first African American on the ASU football team and he graduated from the Journalism Department at ASU.

This paper was to be written for one simple fact. Little Rock Central High is trying to preserve history in every way possible. Not every event occurred at Central, but every event dealt with civil rights and the struggle that many people went through.

One story that stuck in my mind from the interview was about Lee Roy Grant's "welcome to the job" lunch. Bob and Lee Roy were going to go have lunch in order to celebrate Lee Roy getting the job. He was the first black man to work for Southwestern Bell's PR Department. It was 1974, 17 years after the Central High crisis. Bob wanted to take Lee Roy to the Little Rock Club for lunch. When they got there, Lee Roy noticed that it was all white men. He got extremely nervous, turned around, and started to leave. Bob asked him what he was doing and he explained that it was all white men and they weren't going to let him in. Bob explained that no one had a problem with him being an African American and that it was fine if he went in. Lee Roy was concerned because of the misery he had gone though the past several years. Lee Roy came up with a plan to get in. He already had a black suit on so he was going to put a towel over his arm and act like he was a waiter. Bob tried to explain to him that it wasn't necessary. It took a lot, but finally Lee Roy decided that he would trust Bob and go in as a normal person. As Lee Roy walked in and sat down, he noticed that no one had looked at him strangely. There were many smiles of comfort.

After that lunch, Lee Roy had a different view on life. "He walked down the halls with confidence, his head held high," Bob said. "I, on the other hand, had a better glance from the other side of life. I could understand why Lee Roy was afraid. I don't want people to be put into that position. It's unfair and inhumane. God loves everyone and so should we."

For several hundred years, we have struggled for civil rights. Francis Bellamy wrote the words, "liberty and justice for all" a little over 100 years ago. I think that that quote and this story are related to each other in several ways. I think that Lee Roy Grant was finally understanding that the times had changed and that he was welcome. I think that he realized he was free. Maybe not all things would be just, but they were getting there. He felt like a true American at that point. Lee Roy Grant is a good example of "liberty and justice for all."

I used to think of civil rights as just the stories out of the text books. After hearing about Lee Roy Grant's story, I realize that it is much more than that. People actually have gone through these things. Although it wasn't the Central High Crisis, Birmingham Bus Boycott, *Brown v. Board*, or the Greensboro Sit-in, I realize that this was an event in civil rights history that did have a great impact on several people.

So Why Was It Not "For All"?

There are many things that happened during my interview with Jane Doe. In my opinion, the most interesting part of the interview was when she mentioned the Bismarck March for Equal Rights. "They asked us to go to the schools and pick up our kids, then go inside and lock the doors. The black people were marching and protesting through the streets downtown," she said. She was scared out of her wits and was literally praying for it to end.

Jane Doe grew up in Bismarck, Arkansas and grew up in a neighborhood lived in by only white people. She never even saw an African American until she was seven years old on a bus ride. She grew up, married, and became a housewife. She later got a job at a local schoolhouse and taught there until she opened her own daycare in the 1970s. She later got another job teaching and worked there for many years until she retired in the late 1990s.

Interviewer:
Jonathan Carraway

Interviewee:
Jane Doe

Time Period:
1960s

Location:
Bismarck, AR

Affected Group:
African American

Setting:
Public

The overall purpose of the interview itself was to learn as much as we can about history straight from the source. What better way to gather information than from an eyewitness? There is no better way. You can't get real stories out of textbooks or TV programs. The best way to learn about history is to ask someone who was really there and really saw it. This is why I am typing this essay. It would be almost selfish to hold such vital information to American history to myself.

By far the most memorable story from the entire interview was when she finally started to see changes in civil rights. "The changes I saw were at my husband's work. He worked at Safeway Groceries and carried out the groceries to peoples cars. One time my husband took out some groceries that belonged to a colored family and the people in the parking lot were furious. They went to him and attempted to grab the cart from him. When he resisted, they all gathered around him and attempted to assault him. He grabbed the family and told them to follow him. He ran inside the grocery store and locked the doors. They had to wait for the police to arrive to calm them down."

The events that happened changed Jane Doe forever. She tells this in her own words: "At the time I was very scared. Now, looking back on it though I say they have every right to march and demonstrate like they did. They were treated very wrong. If you can't even take out your groceries without getting attacked, what is the point of following the laws at all? It did change me though. Before the Civil Rights Movement, I was very prejudiced, but afterwards I saw that they were people too and should be treated just like us. We have no right treating them like that just because of the color of our skin. We have no right to attack a man trying to help them. I am truly ashamed of myself for how I used to feel toward them."

This incident was very important to the entire Civil Rights Movement. Even though it is only one moment in the entire history of the United States of America, it could be one of the most important. Aren't the last words of the Pledge of Allegiance, "liberty and justice for all"? So why was it not "for all"? So why didn't it apply to African Americans? Even though it was just one incident, there where many more across the USA, and small incidents add up. These events were all one big part of a greater movement. It was a movement called the Civil Rights Movement that changed the way the US looked at African Americans forever. Overall, it put and end to segregation and "separate but equal" in the US.

This interview also changed the way I looked at the Civil Rights Movement. At first it wasn't really a big deal. I knew it was there, but never really stop to think about it. This Memory Project really opened my eyes. Instead of just glancing and saying O.K., I actually took the time to research it and found out so much more than I thought there was to the Civil Rights Movement. Now, I treat the subject with the respect that it deserves and see that it might just be one of the most important parts of US history that there is.

I Just Went Along With It; In Order to Practice Medicine, I Had To

William "Bill" Weaver was 34 years old when integration occurred. He was working as a doctor in Eudora, Arkansas. He is my grandfather and I interviewed him about this time period over the telephone.

"I just went along with it; in order to practice medicine I had to." My grandfather integrated his medical offices as Central High integrated. "It was really different," he stated. "I had the separate bathrooms and waiting rooms for blacks and whites. When I integrated my offices, I switched the signs to just men and women. And even though I did that, the blacks and whites still went to the same ones, disregarding the signs." He said some of the white patients would get angry or impatient when they had to wait in line behind a black person.

> **Interviewer:**
> Selena Nelson
>
> **Interviewee:**
> Dr. William J. Weaver
>
> **Time Period:**
> 1960s
>
> **Location:**
> Eudora, AR
>
> **Affected Group:**
> African American
>
> **Setting:**
> School

"School was a lot different for my children, not really for my older daughter, but really for my son." His son (my uncle) is named Michael. "Michael had been bullied by the black kids because he was white." One time the kids saw Michael driving his motorcycle and they chased him down and knocked him off. The schools had just integrated and there were barely any black kids at school. The next year the school was almost 50 percent black. "My kids had to go through bullying for two years until we decided to move them to private school." He said that the biggest difference between the schools was that one became less safe for some children.

"The neighborhood changed a lot," my grandfather explained to me when the neighborhood was integrated. He said that with all the people that disagreed with integration, there was more crime and vandalism. "I was robbed two times while the beginning of integration had started. Since I was more accepting to the blacks, some white people were mad at me for not standing up or rebelling. Because I was the only doctor in Eudora or any of that area, for a long time, some of my family's safety precautions had to be raised." My grandfather's family had to have a National Guard member live at their house. Sometimes the Guardsman had to walk my mom and uncle to school. Many people moved out of the neighborhood and moved to Louisiana, which was only about 10 minutes away.

Today, my grandfather is 82 years old and he's retired now. I think that integration was the right choice because the Declaration of Independence says that all men are created equal. If we treated the black people with less respect and dignity, then that would be going against everything we believe in. The Declaration of Independence doesn't say all white men were created equal, it says *all* men. I think my grandfather made the right decision by not rebelling and letting it go. To this day, he still thinks integration is O.K. and he always tries to be fair. I'm proud of him for not being ignorant or uncaring.

I've learned a lot from this interview. I learned how the neighborhoods had changed a lot from how they were and how the schools changed. I also learned a lot from my grandfather because he had to make hard decisions when put into situations between friends and beliefs. He had to be very mature about the stuff people were getting into, and to just concentrate on his practice. And last, but not least, I learned that no matter what time period, place, color, social standard, gender, or age, you have to respect everyone, even if you don't have the same beliefs.

Trouble in Selma

My grandfather was a correspondent for the *New York Times* during the Civil Rights Movement. His first major assignment for the newspaper was in 1965 covering Selma, Alabama. He was living in Atlanta at the time. It was at the time when black people were campaigning to vote. That sounds strange today, but back then, large numbers of black people could not vote.

The leaders of the campaign were Dr. Martin Luther King, Jr., and his group and a group made up of college students. On Sunday, March 7, 1965, about 100 black residents of Selma marched from Selma to Montgomery,

Interviewer:	Vincent Reed
Interviewee:	Roy Reed
Time Period:	1960s
Location:	Alabama
Affected Group:	African American
Setting:	Public

Alabama, which was a long way, about 50 miles. These residents made it to about the Alabama River, near the Edmund Pettus Bridge.

They were met by a large number of Alabama State Police troopers. Every officer was armed with guns and billy clubs. The police ordered the marchers to stop, and they did. The marchers were led by one of Martin Luther King's assistants, one of them being Josea Williams. The college student group was led by the Reverend John Lewis. The police then ordered the marchers to stop and head back to Selma. The marchers stayed a while trying to talk it over with the police.

Suddenly, the police all pulled out gas masks. These police were on horseback. The commander then signaled the troopers to move forward, and they did and threw tear gas canisters into the group of marchers. My grandfather was with the reporters and cameras and he said he could hardly breathe and couldn't see a thing. The marchers got it worse because the tear gas was thrown directly at them.

Moments later, the marchers were all coughing and gasping for air. After that the police rushed through on their horses and started swinging their clubs and the commanders had horsewhips and were whipping the marchers. The policemen were beating the black Selma residents. The marchers that were on their feet began running back to Selma as fast as they could, panicking. There were people falling everywhere being knocked unconscious. My grandfather walked over to a couple of people lying on the ground. One of them was Reverend John Lewis. He found out later that he had cracked his skull. My grandfather followed the marchers back to Selma where they gathered at a black church to settle down.

As you would imagine, this incident caused a national scandal. The cameramen that were there caught it all on tape. The next day my grandfather had a story on the front page of the *New York Times*. The country was in an uproar about what happened in Selma.

Within the next couple of days, Martin Luther King gave a very moving speech and Lyndon Johnson went on the air to announce what happened. The next day a woman was killed in her car by the Ku Klux Klan.

I think this is important to civil rights because this incident showed how badly black people were treated back then and how things have changed since the '50s and '60s. After this incident, President Johnson signed a law saying blacks could vote.

He Stuck His Nose Right in the Middle

This interview with my grandfather took place in the little one-story house in San Jose, California he shares with my grandmother. We had the interview in their little kitchen. Since I have been visiting my grandparents, the kitchen has always been my favorite room with the warm California sun seeping through the windows. I could still smell the scent of Grandma's pancakes in the air. As we started the interview, there were the usual sounds of Grandma's house: doors opening and closing as kids were parading through, the sound of the TV being watched, and the constant hum of birds and bees outside. I sat facing my grandfather. He had set a few documents and photos of his story between us. We were ready to begin.

Interviewer:
Alexandra McGough

Interviewee:
Daniel McGough

Time Period:
1960s

Location:
California

Affected Group:
Hispanic American

Setting:
Workplace, Neighborhoods

My grandfather and I were the only two people in the interview. Though, we were never officially alone. Throughout the interview I did not ask any specific questions, just listened to Grandpa's amazing story. He brought up the fact that he was interested in housing development for minorities quite a few times. The particular thing that refuses to leave my mind is that he could have just ignored everything and done nothing, but instead he stuck his nose right in the middle and made something of himself.

Now for the story-telling part of the interview, most of my grandfather's work was in California. He did this during the years of 1964-1968. He was with many people who had the same view. He supported and worked for political candidates who activated the passage of civil rights legislation. He was also helping minorities through tough times.

My grandfather got interested in the California movement to end housing discrimination (wherein some certain areas were "redlined" by real estate interests to keep out minorities). He did this by helping pass the California ballot measure the made housing discrimination illegal. This was his first area of work.

One of the most interesting parts of my grandfather's "journey" was that he worked in the United Farm Worker's Union that was led by Cesar Chavez and was strongly backed by Robert F. Kennedy. This union represented largely Mexican grape pickers in the Salinas Valley of California. These people were given the worst places to live which they had to pay for along with their own food. They could only gain little amounts of money by working a laborious 14 hours a day. My grandfather marched and picketed. Eventually, he got people's attention and in the end gave their union certified so that it could raise their living standards. This was his second area of work.

Toward the end of the interview my grandfather said, "For me, personally, the Civil Rights Era ended the night Robert Kennedy was murdered..." This date was June 6, 1968. This was really how the conflict ended for him.

My grandfather didn't have any strong reactions to his actions or those of others. His main reaction is that he knows the Civil Rights Movement isn't officially over. He thought that his effort was a great opportunity to do the right thing. He said with great pride (probably because he could have just walked by but didn't), "Since it was basically a grass-roots effort, it was easy to get involved in it."

He was not changed greatly. He saw that the "... political winds were reversing." He believes that we will continue to make progress for what we have done. One reason this sticks in my mind is because he had so much will to do this and to continue doing this. My grandfather felt the "Civil Rights Era was a natural evolution to the growth of our democracy and an atonement for our past sins of slavery and discrimination." The thing is, is that he could have just sat by and done nothing. If he had done this his life probably wouldn't have been affected.

This story is important because it shows that one man who was just like thousands of others, made the difference a thousand can make. There is a good and important reason others should notice this story. This reason is that even though it may not seem like someone is making a difference, that one person is doing a world of good.

Marching Through Water

Earline Prince is the most interesting and wise woman I know. She has participated in civil rights demonstrations, became an ordained minister, joined the army, and has done more with her life than most people could dream of. She currently works at the *Arkansas Democrat Gazette*, as a colleague with my mother, Cary Jenkins, and it is here that I met her and became so close to her. But Ms. Earline is more to me than a good friend, she is a role model, a mentor, and she is living history, and that is why I wanted to document her story. Having grown up in Alabama, racism was a built-in part of her world as she continually experienced it first-hand.

> **Interviewer:**
> Jennifer Perren
>
> **Interviewee:**
> Earline Prince
>
> **Time Period:**
> 1960s
>
> **Location:**
> Little Rock, AR
>
> **Affected Group:**
> African American
>
> **Setting:**
> School

What I gathered from her throughout the interview was that racism as I knew it was something different to me than it is to her, because of the fact that that I didn't grow up around it and haven't really, truly experienced it. In other words, my textbook definitions and stories could never compare to the real life situations that Ms. Earline had grown up with.

The recording starts off with Ms. Earline eating her lunch and telling my mom and me stories about when she was younger, mainly about how she stole a fork from a restaurant that only served white folks. It's a funny and enjoyable story, but it was such a small fragment of the extreme stories she was about to release upon me, I was hardly prepared for all the new information.

Starting with her childhood, we built our way through her life until we had covered all her major experiences dealing with racial discrimination, bigotry, and intolerance. At the mere age of seven, she participated in the infamous children's marches of Birmingham that went on in the 1960s. She told about how the older children came and rallied all the younger children up and out of the schools. She described how there was a "sea" of children, so many that the police couldn't stop the influx of children into the streets. As the story goes, the policemen and firemen didn't treat the children reasonably, blasting them with water hoses so strong that it bruised many, and tore the clothes off of others. Eventually, the authorities brought out the dogs and that is when people started to get bitten and mauled. I asked Ms. Earline what her most vivid memory was, and you could see on the video screen the thoughts and memories turning and whirling in her head, and after a moment she answered, "The dogs," and it was obviously a disturbing memory for her. After she recovered she explained, "I just don't understand how anyone could do, or "sick" a dog on somebody else…"

She continued to tell me about her other experiences, some good, and some very bad until our time ran out and I turned the camera off. I was so surprised about all the things I had learned about Ms. Earline in that seemingly small amount of time, I knew I wouldn't be able to ever look at her the same way again. The interview made me stop and think about our nation's history in a way I hadn't before. I had read about slavery and the Civil Rights Movement in books, watched countless documentaries on PBS and heard interviews on the radio, but I always felt sort of disconnected from the real experience. Hearing my friend Ms. Earline tell me such personal, historically significant stories really brought me into American history and gave me a form of connection between my lifetime, and the lives of the people who lived many years before me. I learned through my interview with Earline Prince that textbook explanations and definitions aren't enough when it comes to understanding how people felt about different historical events that they themselves lived through.

Lost Hope

When I was first assigned the Memory Project, I felt rather uncertain I would be able to find anyone that would share their experiences during the Civil Rights Movement with me. My parents had moved to the United States in the late 1980s, decades after any racism, segregation, or important Civil Rights Movements had taken place. It came to my surprise when my father told me that he had taken part in major struggle over civil rights back in China. The 1989 Tiananmen Square protests had marked an important turning point in my father's life, and he was more than willing to share his experiences with me.

Interviewer:	John Doe
Interviewee:	John Doe
Time Period:	1990s
Location:	Beijing, China
Affected Group:	Chinese
Setting:	Public

Later that same sunny afternoon, he and I sat at a homely kitchen table. On one side was me, with pencil and paper, and on the other was my father, a slightly balding middle-aged man dressed in a casual business shirt as always. It was quiet all throughout the house, as though everyone and everything had momentarily paused to listen to this one historical experience. I too waited for a few minutes as he gathered his thoughts, and then began the interview.

"I was a graduate student at Qinghua University in Beijing," he tells me. Ever since the Communist Party took control of China six decades ago, the individual rights of the Chinese citizens have been constricted and slowly drained. These rights include the freedom of speech and press, rights that are guaranteed to all American citizens by the Constitution.

The topics and purpose of this conversation were mainly focused on the background and aftermath of the 1989 Tiananmen Square protests. My father concentrated on the daily aspect and his experiences of the protests, how he had attended nearly every day, arriving at various times in the afternoon and leaving late at night, as well as the last few days of the protests that had lead up to the final devastation which eradicated many of the protestors. Most of the time, he would simply continue his story, occasionally addressing some of the questions that I had posed to him throughout the interview.

One thing that had particularly stuck in my mind throughout the interview was the sense of solemn calmness my father portrayed. As he talked about all the events that essentially composed his earlier life, he carried out a tone that seemed to represent a mixture of all the feelings that were with him at the moment. At times, his expressions would be clouded with slight weariness and sorrow as he further plunged into his memories, but overall his voice was no less passive.

One year after the death of former Secretary General Hu Yaobang, a reformer who had called for anti-corruption within the Chinese government, hundreds of thousands of students gathered at Tiananmen Square in memorial. My father remembers marching from Qinghua University to Tiananmen Square, shouting slogans asking for anti-corruption and change. These protests began occurring more frequently, and by May [a month later], all schools had been closed because students no longer attended class.

After weeks of protests and hunger strikes, the Chinese government had finally agreed to talk with the student delegates. Their meeting was broadcasted on television. My father recalls how some of the delegates were so weak from hunger that they had to wear oxygen tanks. The government accused the previous demonstrations as being illegal and told the students they should let the government "do their job." At those words, my father had felt infuriated. In order to show they were not intimidated by the government, an even larger group of people, this time comprised not only of students, but teachers, factory workers, and restaurant managers, marched to Tiananmen Square. Conflict began later in the day, when the Chinese government announced they were sending soldiers to take control of Beijing. In an effort to prevent the soldiers from coming in, my father and several others lied down on the majors streets, blocking the path of the military trucks. He had even talked to the soldiers, telling them how the protestors were not extremists, but simply wanted reformation. All seemed well for now, as the Chinese government looked as though they had given up. But my father learned later that the protestors' increased denial and rebellion against the Chinese government had ignited an even larger flame of conflict and tension.

On the night of June 3, my father had left the protest and went over to his uncle's house to spend the night. Later, he heard on the radio that the Chinese government was going to send troops to Tiananmen Square and remove all protestors by force, and everyone was told to remain inside. Concern began to grow in my father. Despite this warning, most of the protestors had still remained in Tiananmen Square. Even at his uncle's house a few miles away, my father could still hear the constant gunshots as they rained upon the night.

My father rode on his bicycle early in the morning to Tiananmen Square to see what had happened. Soldiers were marching everywhere with loaded rifles. "The way they looked, they were going to shoot or attack anybody," he said. On the street, he saw several dead bodies lined up, with their upper bodies covered. He was told by someone else that those protestors had been run over by a tank. Anger and grief began to overwhelm my father.

My father's experience of Tiananmen Square left a silent affliction in his life. His opinion of the Chinese government had changed, as he felt they were not helpers of the country, but rather "dictators and murderers, killing unarmed students." A year later, my father came to the United States. His decision was primarily made in order to flee the persecution the Chinese government had begun enforcing upon any protestors who had survived the massacre. Furthermore, he felt that after the incident, he had "lost hope for Chinese democracy."

This interview with my father has allowed me to recognize the importance of civil rights. His struggles have helped me to understand and appreciate the freedoms that have already been bestowed upon us, and realize that even today, many countries far and wide, are still fighting the same battle of liberty and equality that we did less than two centuries ago.

Words of Change
Mallory Jeffers

Afterword

Stories have existed longer than anything tangible or material that has been fashioned by man. The first humans told stories to transmit vital survival information. This primitive form of oral history passed instructions about killing beasts, where to find water, what to kill, and why some seasons were better than others. As time progressed, we started to use metaphors and symbolism in our stories. By then, we had figured out how to kill enough animals and grow enough food that the new problem for survival was learning to live together peacefully. Complex forms of speech and theories were developing. With that development, opinions and problems within communities began to arise. Therefore, the first laws and moral codes were embedded in stories and transmitted to each generation through anecdotes told orally. The overall function of stories never changed. Even though we now tend to say that stories have "morals" or "lessons," they are still instructions about learning how to survive. Stories still function as survival tools.

So, naturally, our first goal with this book was to show the importance of oral history in our lives. Ever since starting the project, we've heard from students whose essays were used for this book that they've been able to open up new lines of communication with their family because of the interview. Adam Thannisch mentioned how he'd formed a deeper connection with his grandfather because of the interview he performed. Brenna Gilstrap's interview with her grandfather was the last recording of his voice before he had multiple debilitating strokes. Lincoln Munro's son found his father's story on the Central High Memory Project webpage, and it revealed to him how little he knew of his father and prompted him to find out more.

These new connections are visible in nearly every essay—look for the mention of how they never knew their parents or their grandparents were involved in demonstrations or were witnesses to horrible things.

This project has the potential to help people our age connect with their elders and help preserve the oral tradition. Today, connections with family are undervalued. People get entertainment from just about everything except communication with their family—we're more likely to sit down and watch an episode re-run of *Seinfeld* or *Fresh Prince of Bel-Air* than tell a story about grandpa.

This book also has the ability to show what the students think and how much they know about the history that they come in contact with. Their phrasings and choice of words betray what they think and feel about political correctness and the Civil Rights Movement. The gaps and omissions show what they don't yet know, and if they fail to pursue a line of questioning that might have been fruitful, it simply shows their inexperience in the learned art of interviewing.

The essays themselves are reflective of the writers: the shapes they take end up showing what the writer thought and knew of the history and of their interviewee at the time they talked. One of the goals of the Memory Project book is to show what students can learn and *have* learned from listening to these personal experience stories. We think these essays, with all their flaws and successes, do show this.

Our sponsor teachers would continually ask us, "What makes an essay important enough for others to read?"

This question of importance continually popped up both in the selection and the editing stages of the book. It was important to our job. If there was an actual standard we could use, a grade system that would let us choose which essays to put in, then all we'd have to do is grade the essays and the job of selection would be done for us. It wasn't that easy, of course.

The gaps in our selection process became more apparent as we went ahead (and again, we encourage you all to visit the Central High Memory Project Website and see the rest of the essays for yourself). New essays would sometimes appear that had been left out by some readers, and our teachers would insist that they were important. They sometimes would deal with a personal story in a concise manner but be almost too short, and sometimes they would deal with an incredibly obscure event. One dealt with a small piece of local history, but without the context, the reader couldn't understand it.

One answer to the importance question was, of course, readability. But, in many cases, this excluded less competent writers, or essays that only approached a point instead of making one, or essays without a compelling narrative. If the essay was well-written, even then, it wasn't necessarily important. The idea of "the exceptional" cropped up. Basically, if the essay was exceptional in some way (if it made a good point, if it had an especially compelling narrative), then it was important enough for others to read. What it boiled down to though, was another, subjective question: "Does the essay "feel" special?"

For us as a team, we'd like for you to consider this, and other questions, as you reflect on this book: What makes oral histories important? What can be learned from isolated stories without broader, historical context? What do you think contributed to racism, what contributed to the eventual change? What more can you do to further equality? How inclusive should civil rights be? What groups do you think should be included and what rights should they get? How do you make attitudes more tolerant?

As you find your answers to questions like these, then you will be able to join us in thinking about our beginning question: What makes an essay important enough for others to read?

We would like to help expand the oral tradition in this country. The past is neglected here, and children more often than not fail to form meaningful connections with their elders. This book, hopefully, helps show what a waste this is and, by contrast, what can happen when you try.

We want to encourage the making of these connections. Meanwhile, for those who do, our next step is to create a template for our Memory Project website that you can use to build an oral history in your own community.

The Central High Memory Project Editing Team
May 2009

Tree of Life/Death and Separation
Myriah Downs

Discussion Questions

After reading essays selected for this book, Central students were invited to create questions they wanted to ask other people who read the book. That includes their classmates today, Central students in the future, students in other schools, teachers, parents and older adults—in other states and in other countries. Here's our list of things to think about:

"Dear Reader,
After reading the essays in this book…"

Do you think Central has changed since 1957?

Is history happening around us? How can we be more attentive to it?
How are the struggles for equality the same and different worldwide?

What are the criteria for being treated equally?
Do the oppressed people of the past have the right to seek revenge today?

Can you relate to any of the instances of prejudice mentioned in the book?
Have you ever been unfairly treated by an authority figure without an opportunity to defend yourself?
Have you ever been bullied? Can you imagine having a whole race bully you?
Can you think of a time that you stereotyped someone or were stereotyped yourself based on religion, skin color, or a disability?

Is your school completely accepting and fair?
How might your teachers justify their biases?
How are racial slurs taken in the conversations around you?
What does a person's socio-economic status mean to you?

How is interracial dating viewed? Why is it often discouraged?

After 911, did you find yourself suspicious of Muslims or Middle Easterners?
How is prejudice instilled by politicians?
How does the media instigate ideas of intolerance?

Why can the discussion of segregation and prejudice be uncomfortable for some people?
Why are people shy to admit the flaws in our current society in terms of racism and segregation?
How would you participate in such a conversation?

How were you brought up to view "others" – people who are physically different than you?
Have you ever thought of prejudice from the opposite point of view?
It has been said that "Racism is still engraved the in the older generation"; is this true? What about the younger generation?

What is racism and who does it affect?
What causes people to discriminate against other races?
How have the structures of racism changed over time?
Do you think prejudices will continue to shift? Why?
Knowing this, what are you doing to inspire change?
What barriers do you have to break down now?
Is it always necessary to act and break those barriers? Are you always the one to do it?

Have you practiced nonviolence? Has any one tried to stop you?
Is violence ever necessary?
Are you willing to fight as hard as the activists for your beliefs?
As an activist, would an arrest stop you?

Would you tell your grandchildren your story?
Even with all of our efforts, is it possible to actually eliminate prejudice?

Credits

Cover Art
Shariq Ali, *original artwork: "Awkward Penetration," charcoal*
Mackie O'Hara, *cover concept and design*
H. K. Stewart, *cover design consultant*
Rex Deloney, *consultation in conjunction with the LRCHS Art Department*

Editors-in-Chief
As active members of every team throughout the project, these two students volunteered to take responsibility for organizing student volunteers, identifying tasks to be completed by each production team, and coordinating the work of each team throughout the stages of the project. In addition to reading every essay considered by the Reading Team, they served as final proofreaders for the editing of the 75 essays selected. When the work of the other editing teams was completed, they spent an additional two weeks during the summer collaboratively writing the final versions of the Foreword, Afterword, and chapter commentaries.

Mackie O'Hara
Alex Richardson

Editing Team

The work done by the Editing Team really brought this book together in terms of organization and vision. Working daily, during and after school, these students read and reread all of the selected essays and determined what made the stories "important enough" for other people to read. Many afternoons were devoted almost entirely to that question and brought about meaningful discussions which flowed into the chapter structure of the book. Groups within the team indexed essays by topic, identified recurring themes, collected author release forms, selected student artwork, and drafted commentaries for essays and chapters.

Muhammad Abu-Rmaileh
Hamza Arshad
Sarah Evans
Clayton Gentry
Magdalene James
Sarah Kline
Aya Kondo
Josh Lintag
Sarah Lintag

Siteng Ma
Ghassan Makhoul
James Nunnley
Chelsi Page
Sydney Sloan
Khaylin Williams
Tashayla Withers
Yi Wu
Aaron Yin

Reading Team

Students who became members of the Reading Team volunteered to read 30-50 essays on the Memory Project website, identified those essays they thought were "especially important for others to read," and wrote recommendations for the essays selected. These students did their work after school.

Livingston Anderson
Autumn Brown
Kaelin Bullock
Amanda Carreiro
Ascha Fairmon
Catherine Fox
Zack Johnson
Helio Liu
Jane Madden
Ritika Mazumder

Tatenda Mukunyadzi
Kierra Porter
Bianca Reece
Rachel Roberts
Nicole Sullivan
Alexis Taylor
Joshua (J. T.) Taylor
Helen Wilson
Bob Zhao

Question Teams

Several teachers devoted one or more class periods to this activity. Students worked in reading circles or individually to generate questions for use in the Discussion Questions section of the book. The students listed below read 5-10 selected essays, wrote comments about their personal reactions to the essays, and then wrote a "guiding question" for other readers to use for reflection on particular stories or life experiences re-told in the essays.

Ms. Celeste Archer's 9th grade Civics class:

Tavelyn Allen
Aline Bernal
Chastity Carrothers
Harnechia Conway
Haley Cooper
George Elrod
Tylah Floyd
Abby Gatmaitan
Barrett Goodwin
Brennan Henson

Xavier Jones
Tyneshia Lee
Janie Blair Luft
Daniel Massirer
Christina Nguyen
Janie Ruffins
Zach Wilson
Andrew Wise
Anna Zerull

Mr. Scott Hairston's 12th grade English class:

Dijon Britton
Winnfield Brooks
Felicia Derry
Whiney Fears
Jasmin Fernandez
Ayanna Ganaway
Julie Haralson
Keyjahjna Hayes
Jarvis Hines
Jonathan Matlock
Olivia Muldrew

Darian Quiles
London Reid
Bobby Russell
Christopher Scott-Cline
Hummad Tasneem
Sean Turner
Keylon Tyler
Susan Van Ness
Allen-Michael Ward
Brittany Watkins

Mr. Keith Richardson's 9th grade Civics/12th grade Geography classes:

Tamara Abulez
Justin Bryles
Kaelin Bullock
Briana Carter
Lance Cummings
Daneele Dickerson
Kashaf Malik
Jordan McWilliams

Chandani Patel
Trinity Randolph
Ciara Schroeder
Lane Siems
Maggie Thannisch
Dasha Tippen
Britney Washington
Morgan Williamson

Mr. George West's 9th grade Civics classes:

Suzanne Abou Diab
Demiko Adams
Claire Adney
Anton Alexeev
Rachel Anderson
Anna Anglin
Summer Ashley
Jaden Atkins
Maryssa Barron
Caitlin Bowe
Michael Bower
Sadie Bullard
John Clement
Anthony Cloird
Kelvin Coleman
Alyssa Davis
Kristena Dyer
Clayton Gentry
Shree Govindarajan
Madison Greenfield
Jake Haley
Josh Hammons
Tyniesha Hampton
Thomas Horn
Yakeisha Jenkins
Danielle Kensington

Adam Kirosingh
Aya Kondo
Karle Lawson
Randy Lee
Jane Madden
Andrew Martin
Madison Matthews
Ritika Mazumder
Callie Meeker
Tatenda Mukunyadzi
Baird Newbern
Eric Nichols
Patrick Olive
Amy Page
Anna Parker
Everett Pilcher
Salma Santoyo
Claire Schmidt
Jason Seo
Addie Smith
Macy Stanley
Mackenzie Thompson
Taylor Thompson
Chara Turner
Mindy Ware
Noah Whitney

Mr. George West's 10th-12th grade Voices of Civil Rights/Oral History Research class:

Isaiah Bailey	Sara Stewart
Maritza Chora	Kerric Turner
Olivia Dockery	Jalin Wesley
Ebony Ellison	Lazandra Williams
Shaylonda Jackson	Shaela Williams

Student Artists

The artwork of these students was selected by the Editing Team to illustrate chapter themes in the book. Their art was originally created in art classes at Central High for the 50th Commemoration exhibit entitled "Looking Back, Looking Ahead." The Editing Team sifted through the works of the exhibit and chose the works of these artists.

Shariq Ali	Tony Hughes
David Aspesi	Mallory Jeffers
Jessica Boyd	Sophie King
Melody Chang	Jennifer Perren
Ross Cooper	Rae Plugge
Myriah Downs	Allie Thompson
Gabriel Goldman	Samuel Weekley
Andrew Hamby	

Website Founders

Members of the first Memory Project Team created the website as a way to archive the oral histories collected by the students. After researching the oral history collections at the Library of Congress, they designed the themes and categories used to index the essays, created the initial version of Memory Project website, and served as "griot" storytellers to share the stories collected and to present the project to public audiences.

Cameron Zohoori, *Editor-in-Chief*	Melody Chang
	Max Farrell
Adam Kelleher, Site Design, *Webmaster*	Gary Li
	Tafi Mukunyadzi
Daisha Booth	Lauren Wright
Bailey Brosh	Anne Ye

Faculty

These members of the Central High faculty supervise students in planning and taping interviews, writing and posting essays for the Memory Project website, and producing dramatic interpretation, art exhibits, and community presentations.

Art Team
Rex Deloney
Jason McCann
Lynn Smith
Nancy Wilson

Civics Team
Mike Johnson
Adam Kirby
Cynthia Mahomes Nunnley
Keith Richardson
George West

Drama Team
Kim Dade
Agnolia Gay

English Team
Scott Hairston
Sharolyn Jones-Taylor
Sarah Schutte

Technology Team
April Rike
Kirby Shofner

Sponsors

These organizations have provided funds and/or publicity in support of research and planning, curriculum development and professional training for the teaching teams, opportunities for students with interviewing projects, website development, public performance, community outreach, and publications of Memory Project research and lesson plans.

National Park Service, Little Rock Central High School Historic Site Visitors Center
Little Rock Public Education Foundation
Best Buy Corporation, Teach Grant
Marie Foundation, Spitzberg Family
National Women's History Association
American Historical Association
Arkansas Historical Association
Teaching Tolerance, Southern Poverty Law Center
Little Rock Central High PTSA
Learn and Serve America
Corporation for National and Community Service
Arkansas Department of Education

Kick Start the Year
Tony Hughes

Appendices:

Timeline
1954-59 School Desegregation

Lesson Plans
Memory Project Interview Guide
Memory Project Taping Do's and Don'ts
Editing Team Reflection Assignment
Reading Team Discussion Questions

Timeline:
1954-59 School Desegregation

Events in the desegregation of Central High offer an ideal case study of American Civics. The rule of law, representative democracy, the separation of powers into three branches, the system of checks and balances to prevent abuse of power—the basic topics are all there. So are equally fundamental but more complex concepts: the guarantee of equal protection under the law, the preservation of minority rights alongside the principle of majority rule, and the historical tensions between federal authority and states' rights in our system of federalism. Most importantly, this timeline underscores the essential ingredient that makes America's democracy work: civic responsibility. The lead characters in the Central High story, at the beginning and again at the end, are the citizens who take action. First it is the local chapter of the NAACP and the Little Rock Nine and their families who insist on their right to equal access to the best public education. Then, in the Lost Year, it is the Women's Emergency Committee (WEC) and the STOP campaign (Stop This Outrageous Purge) who succeed in re-opening Little Rock's high schools after a recall election against school board members who arrogantly had fired teachers supportive of desegregation. In these events of the past, students today can readily observe the power and responsibility that falls on them as citizens if they want their government to live up to its promise of liberty and justice for all. —Teachers' Note

1954

17 May—The *Brown v. Board of Education* decision is handed down by the U.S. Supreme Court, unanimously ruling that state laws mandating public school segregation are unconstitutional under the equal-protection clause of the 14th Amendment. The high court rejects the "separate but equal" doctrine in force since its *Plessy v. Ferguson* ruling of 1896, declaring that segregated schools "are inherently unequal."

22 May—The LRSD Board of Directors issues a policy statement asserting that the Little Rock School District would comply with the Supreme Court decision when methods and timelines are made available.

23 August—Eleven black children join 480 white students in the schools of Charleston, Ark., making it the first community in Arkansas (and the first in the former Confederate South) to integrate its schools. Administrators do not publicly make an announcement about the successful integration for three weeks, thus avoiding a media frenzy.

7 September—Fayetteville High School enrolls nine black students along with its 500 white students, following Charleston as the second desegregated system in Arkansas.

1955

24 May—The LRSD Board of Directors and Superintendent Virgil T. Blossom issue a plan of gradual integration for Little Rock schools (known as the "Blossom Plan"), beginning with the high schools, then the junior high schools, and finally the elementary schools. The integration will begin in 1957.

11 July—Twenty-five black students enroll peacefully amid 1,000 white students in Hoxie, the third Arkansas school system to desegregate and the first in an area of the state with a substantial black population.

20 August—Mounting white opposition to integration in Hoxie, following a story in *Life*, leads the local board to close its schools.

24 October—Hoxie schools reopen after a federal court bars segregationists from preventing the admission of blacks. Widespread white absenteeism is reported.

1956

8 February—The NAACP files a lawsuit against the Little Rock School District, claiming that 33 African-American children were denied admittance to white schools (*Aaron v. Cooper*).

28 August—The NAACP suit is dismissed. Federal Judge John E. Miller declares that the School Board is acting "in utmost good faith" to set an integration plan in motion. The NAACP appeals the decision.

6 November—Voters approve three anti-integration measures: Amendment 47 (directing the legislature to create laws opposing *Brown v. Board of Education*); a Resolution of Interposition establishing a state policy of segregation; and Initiated Act 2, a pupil assignment law.

1957

19 February—The Arkansas Senate passes four pro-segregation bills: creation of the State Sovereignty Commission; removal of the mandatory school attendance requirement at integrated schools; a requirement for the registration of certain individuals and organizations; and the authorization of school boards to use school funds to fight against integration. Governor Orval Faubus signs all four bills.

16 March—Wayne Upton and Henry V. Rath are elected to the LRSD Board of Directors by conclusive margins over the two segregationist candidates in their respective zones. Both Upton and Rath endorse the gradual integration plan.

27 April—The 8th Circuit U.S. Court of Appeals in St. Louis upholds Judge Miller's dismissal of the NAACP suit.

30 August—Federal District Judge Ronald N. Davies orders the School Board to proceed with its integration of Little Rock Central High School on the opening day of school (September 3). Judge Davies enjoins "all persons in any manner, directly or indirectly," from interfering with the integration plan.

2 September—The National Guard surrounds Central High on orders from Governor Faubus because of "evidence of disorder and threats of disorder." After this act, the School Board instructs the nine black students who have registered to attend Central (and afterwards are known to the world as the "Little Rock Nine") not to attempt to attend school.

3 September—Judge Davies orders that integration begin at Central High School on September 4. Governor Faubus announces that the National Guard will remain at the school.

4 September—The nine students attempt to enter the school but are turned away by the National Guard. Little Rock Mayor Woodrow Mann calls Governor Faubus' claims of threatened violence a hoax. Governor Faubus telegraphs President Dwight D. Eisenhower to stop "unwarranted interference of federal agents."

5 September—President Eisenhower responds to Governor Faubus, saying that the Constitution will "be upheld by every legal means" and requests "full co-operation to the United States District Court." The School Board asks for temporary suspension of the integration plan.

7 September—Judge Davies denies the School Board's request for temporary suspension of the integration plan. He orders integration to begin on September 9.

8 September—Governor Faubus goes on national television to re-affirm his stand against integration and insists that the federal government back off. He calls himself "the preservator of the peace," but declines to produce any hard evidence of reported violence over the issue.

9 September—Judge Davies directs federal authorities to bring proceedings against Governor Faubus and the National Guard officers to prevent them from interfering with the integration of Central High School.

14 September—Governor Faubus meets with President Eisenhower at the vacation White House in Newport, RI.

20 September—Judge Davies rules that Governor Faubus did not use the National Guard troops to preserve law and order and forbids him and the National Guard from interfering with integration. Faubus' attorney walks out of the hearing. The governor removes the National Guard from the school in the early evening, ending the 17-day military standoff with the federal government. Little Rock police then move in.

23 September—The Little Rock Nine enter a side door at Central High School as a crowd of about 1,000 whites riots out front. The police cannot handle the crowd. The nine students are removed from the school before noon for their safety. President Eisenhower calls the rioting disgraceful and issues a proclamation paving the way for the use of federal troops to stop it. This day sometimes is referred to as "Black Monday."

24 September—The 101st Airborne Division (1,100 officers and soldiers) rolls into Little Rock. The Arkansas National Guard is placed under federal orders and mobilized, creating a perimeter around Central High School.

25 September—Under troop escort, the nine students ride up to Central High School in an Army staff car and enter the school. A military presence remained for the rest of the school year.

9 October—Governor Faubus states that only the withdrawal of the nine students would end the crisis at Central High School.

26 October—the NAACP files suits in federal District court challenging the validity of Act 83 of 1957 (creating the state Sovereignty Commission) and the Little Rock "Bennett" ordinance (requiring certain organizations to file membership lists and other information).

3 December—Mrs. L.C. (Daisy) Bates, state NAACP president, is fined $100 in Little Rock Municipal Court for failing to comply with the Little Rock "Bennett" ordinance.

17 December—Black student Minnijean Brown dumps a bowl of chili on two of her white antagonists in the Central High cafeteria. She receives a six-day suspension.

29 December—The Public Affairs Committee of Freedom House says in its year-end report that Governor Faubus and Russia's satellites were the two major factors helping to tilt the scales against freedom in 1957.

1958

8 January—Jim Johnson of Crossett, a segregationist, files a comprehensive proposed amendment to the state constitution including a provision by which integrated schools could be closed and sold.

24 January—Five bomb threats in five days occur at Central, but nothing is found except a stick of dynamite without a fuse or cap and a few firecrackers.

14-15 February—Businessman William F. Rector says that New Jersey interests backed out of a proposed $10 million shopping center because of the integration trouble. Governor Faubus denies the allegation; he claims that Rector is an integrationist and a Republican. Rector calls the governor a skunk.

17 February—Minnijean Brown is expelled from Central. She has been involved in more incidents than any of the other black students. Sammie Dean Parker, a white student, is suspended for pushing Gloria Ray, one of the nine, down a flight of stairs; and two white boys are suspended for showing cards saying "One down, eight to go." Minnijean says she is being punished for calling a girl "white trash" after the other girl hit her.

20 March—The Pine Bluff School Board says that it is postponing indefinitely its plans for integration because of the trouble in Little Rock.

25 May—The first African-American student to graduate from Central High School is Ernest Green. Civil rights leader Dr. Martin Luther King, Jr., is in attendance at the ceremony as a guest of the Green family.

3 June—In federal court nine Little Rock school officials testify that the previous year was one of chaos and tension at Central: that the educational program had been disrupted, that an extra financial burden had been placed on the School Board and that the board could see no prospect for improvement if integration were continued in September 1958. The testimony is for a delay of 2-1/2 years for integration in Little Rock.

4 June—As the hearing continues, School Board president Wayne Upton testifies that the January 1961 date chosen to resume integration in Little Rock was selected partly because the board thought Governor Faubus would be out of office by then. Little Rock Superintendent Virgil T. Blossom testifies that the School Board encountered "total opposition" from all three branches of the state government.

21 June—The federal court grants a delay until January 1961 for integration of Little Rock schools (known as the "Lemley delay").

26 June—The NAACP asks the U.S. Supreme Court to bypass the 8th Circuit Appeals Court and take emergency action on the Lemley delay.

30 June—Supreme Court sends the Lemley case back to the Appeals Court for action.

4 August—The Lemley case is argued before the 8th Circuit Court of Appeals.

18 August—The Appeals Court sets aside the Lemley delay order, writing that "the time has not yet come in these United States when an order of a federal court must be whittled away, watered down or shamefully withdrawn in the face of violent and unlawful acts of citizens."

21 August—The Appeals Court stays for 30 days the effect of its order overruling the Lemley delay in order for the School Board to appeal to the Supreme Court. The School Board announces it will open segregated schools on September 21.

23 August—Governor Faubus calls a special session to start August 26 to deal with the integration problem.

25 August—The Supreme Court announces that it will take up the Little Rock integration matter during a special session on August 28. The School Board announces that the start of school will be delayed until September 8.

26 August—Governor Faubus addresses the legislature, saying that the federal government has no power in the integration issue: there are no laws concerning integration and the states did not give that power to the federal government. He offered six proposed laws, including one that would allow him to close the public high schools. An old law still on the books would allow the buildings to be leased out as private schools.

28 August—The Supreme Court delays hearing arguments until September 11.

1 September—The Board of Directors decides to delay the opening of the high schools until September 15 because of the Supreme Court delay, but opens the other schools on time on September 4.

12 September—The Supreme Court decrees unanimously that integration must proceed in Little Rock. Then events occur in the following order:

1. The School Board orders the high schools to open integrated on September 15.
2. One board member, Henry Rath, resigns in protest of the ruling.
3. Governor Faubus signs into law the school closing bill (Act 4).
4. Governor Faubus signs all of the special session legislation.
5. Governor Faubus orders the four high schools (Central, Hall, Technical and Mann) closed as of 8 a.m., September 15.

About 150 special deputy federal marshals arrive in Little Rock to help enforce the Supreme Court's ruling.

The 1958-59 school year, with no classes held in the public high schools, is commonly referred to as "The Lost Year." Approximately 3,400 students were affected by the closing of the high schools.

17 September—With the aid of Governor Faubus, the Little Rock Private School Corporation is incorporated and plans to lease the public school buildings and open private schools. The Women's Emergency Committee to Open Our Schools is formed to solicit votes "for integration" in the special election on September 27.

18 September—Governor Faubus makes an appeal for votes "against integration" in the election. The Private School Corporation says it doesn't know yet how it is going to finance its operations, but it has the promise of state accreditations for its schools.

22 September—The first day of two-hour television classes for Little Rock high school students is deemed a success by most participants. All three local television channels are involved: KATV, the ABC affiliate, broadcast classes for sophomores; KTHV, the CBS affiliate, showed course for juniors; and KARK, the NBC affiliate, broadcast courses for seniors. LRSD superintendent Virgil Blossom said of the televised classes, "At Central High we offer 87 different subjects. On television we're attempting only the four basic subjects—English, history, science and mathematics."

27 September—Votes are 19,470 to 7,561 against "immediate integration of all schools." Governor Faubus says he will act with all dispatch to open the public schools as private schools. The NAACP goes to the Appeals Court to prevent this.

29 September—The School Board leases its closed high schools to the Private School Corporation, but within hours the Appeals Court enjoins the board from going through with the transaction. The Supreme Court says that "evasive schemes for segregation" cannot be used to nullify court orders.

17 October—The Private School Corporation leases a building at 16th and Lewis streets formerly used by the University of Arkansas Graduate Center at Little Rock. This private school will be named T.J. Raney High School. About 750 students will attend Raney. Two additional privately operated facilities—Baptist High School, located at 8th and Scott streets, and Trinity Interim Academy—enroll more displaced high school students.

22 October—Seniors attend their first day of classes at Raney High School, and registration of juniors and sophomores begins.

4 November—Orval Faubus is elected to his third two-year term as governor, garnering 83 percent of the vote against Republican George W. Johnson.

10 November—The three-judge panel of the Appeals Court orders the School Board to take positive steps toward integration on instructions that they will receive from the district judge and also on their own initiative.

12 November—Five School Board members, all but Dr. Dale Alford, vote to buy out Superintendent Virgil T. Blossom's contract, then they resign from the board. They call their position hopeless and helpless. Alford does not resign, but his term will be over on December 6; he has been elected to the state legislature and does not seek re-election to the board.

13 November—A lawsuit is filed in the Chancery Court of Pulaski County to prevent the payment of the buy-out money to Blossom.

15 November—Fifteen candidates file for the School Board election on the final day of eligibility.

17 November—The State Department of Education begins making payments of $24.50 per month per student to schools outside the district for educating Little Rock high school students.

6 December—In the School Board election, three members of the "businessman's" slate (Ted L. Lamb, Everett Tucker, Jr., and Russell H. Matson, Jr.) and three who promise to cooperate with Governor Faubus (Ben Rowland, Sr., Robert W. Laster and Ed I. McKinley) win election.

18 December—Terrell E. Powell, the principal at Hall High School, is appointed Superintendent to succeed Virgil T. Blossom.

22 December—The State Supreme Court upholds the Bennett ordinance on appeal, meaning that the NAACP must open its records. The NAACP says it will appeal the decision.

1959

11 January—District Judge John E. Miller, following the mandate sent down from the Appeals Court, orders the School Board to move forward in carrying out the court-ordered integration plan and to report back in 30 days on its progress.

14 January—T.J. Raney High School receives accreditation as a Class A school from the state Department of Education. It now is eligible to apply for the state aid that is being withheld from the closed public high schools.

4 February—The testimony of Superintendent Terrell Powell in federal court shows that 3,665 high school students have been displaced by the high school lockouts: of 2,915 white students, 1,120 are in private schools in Little Rock and Conway, 877 are in other public schools in Arkansas, 275 are attending schools outside Arkansas and 643 are not in school. Of the district's 750 African-American students, 229 are in public schools in the state, 79 are in school outside the state and 442 are not in school.

6 February—The State Board of Education narrowly decides to pay state aid to T.J. Raney High School under Act 5 of 1958.

26 February—The State Department of Education says it has paid $187,768 of Little Rock's withheld state aid to other Arkansas schools who have been educating Little Rock students.

8 March—The federal court enjoins the state from paying out any more of Little Rock's withheld state aid under Act 5 of 1958.

11 March—Governor Faubus' proposed constitutional amendment (SJR 5), to allow local school districts to abolish their schools by vote to avoid integration, is approved by both houses of the legislature.

22 April—B.T. Shelton, an African-American teacher in Little Rock and a member of the NAACP, files suit in federal court against Act 10 of 1958 and Act 115 of 1959. Act 10 requires teachers to sign affidavits listing all organizational memberships and contributions made in the last five years.

28 April—The Arkansas Supreme Court upholds Act 4 of 1958, the school closing law, by a 4-to-3 margin.

6 May—The School Board splits over the issue of teacher contracts. Half of the members of the board (Ed McKinley, Ben Rowland and Robert Laster), declaring themselves a quorum after the other three board members walk out of a board meeting, vote not to renew the contracts of 44 employees, including seven principals. The Classroom Teachers Association immediately calls the action illegal.

7 May—The PTA Council strongly criticizes the firing of the 44 employees and suggests recall proceedings against the three board members. Mass protest meetings spring up at several schools.

9 May—STOP (Stop This Outrageous Purge) is organized by 179 prominent downtown business and civic leaders for the purpose of recalling McKinley, Rowland and Laster.

10 May—Recall petitions against board members Everett Tucker, Ted Lamb and Russell Matson also are in circulation. The Mothers League of Central High takes credit. In a statement McKinley says most of the 44 employees fired were integrationists but they can have their jobs back if they'll sign statements that they will uphold "the public policy" of segregation.

26 May—STOP makes a clean sweep in the recall election: Tucker, Lamb and Matson are kept on the board; McKinley, Rowland and Laster are voted out.

11 June—The Pulaski County Board of Education appoints three new Little Rock School Board members to replace those recalled by voters. The new members are state Rep. J.H. Cottrell Jr., contractor Henry Lee Hubbard and insurance company official B. Frank Mackey. The reconstituted board rehires 39 of the 44 employees fired on May 5.

18 June—A three-judge U.S. District Court panel declares Act 4, the state's 1958 school-closing law, unconstitutional. The Board of Directors announces that it will not appeal the decision and will reopen the city's high schools in the fall.

21 July—Baptist High's Board of Directors closes the school after one year, citing a lack of students.

4 August—Officials of privately operated Raney High announce that the school will close because it is out of money.

11 August—Governor Faubus goes on television to discourage overt resistance when the high schools reopen. "I see nothing to be gained tomorrow by disorder and violence," he says. Instead, he urges viewers to "go to work and elect some officials who will represent you and not betray you." He emphasizes that he is "not throwing in the sponge."

12 August—Little Rock's four high schools open, nearly a month early. Three black students (Effie Jones, Estella Thompson and Elsie Marie Robinson) enroll at Hall. Two of the original Little Rock Nine (Jefferson Thomas and Elizabeth Eckford) enroll at Central. Eckford finds out that she has enough correspondence-school credits for her diploma and doesn't need to continue classes. Another of the original nine students, Carlotta Walls, enrolls at Central later in the month.

Segregationists rally at the State Capitol where Governor Faubus advises them that it is a "dark day" but they should not give up the struggle. The group then marches to Central High School where the police and fire departments break up the mob. Twenty-one people are arrested.

28 August—Two unidentified women throw two tear-gas bombs inside the front door of the district Administration Building while the School Board is meeting on the second floor. There are no injuries.

7 September—Three dynamite blasts shake the city on Labor Day; nobody is hurt. One blast demolishes a city-owned station wagon parked in the driveway of Fire Chief Gann Nalley's home. Another damages the front of a two-story building housing a construction firm of which Mayor Werner Knoop is vice president. The third detonates at the Little Rock School District Administration Building at Louisiana and 8th streets, wrecking an empty office. Nuns from a nearby convent were able to give the FBI a description of the suspects' car, aiding in the arrests.

9 September—Two Little Rock men (lumber and roofing company owner E. A. Lauderdale and truck driver J. D. Sims) are arrested in the bombings and charged with dynamiting a public building.

10 September—Three more local men are arrested on the same charges. All five defendants are convicted, fined $500 and sentenced to prison terms of three to five years. Testimony indicates that the mastermind is Lauderdale, an active member of the Capital Citizens Council. Lauderdale's prison term is commuted by Governor Faubus after a little more than five months.

Timeline Sources:

Little Rock School District archives.

Arkansas Online: Historic Front Pages from the *Arkansas Gazette* and the *Arkansas Democrat*, online at http://www.ardemgaz.com/prev/central/. Accessed 12 July 2007.

The Lost Year Project, online at http://www.thelostyear.com/index.html. Accessed 13 July 2007.

Little Rock Central High School 40th Anniversary website, online at http://www.centralhigh57.org/. Accessed 9 July 2007.

National Park Service, Little Rock Central High School National Historic Site web page, online at http://www.nps.gov/chsc/index.htm. Accessed 13 July 2007.

"School district employee marks 50 years on job." *Arkansas Democrat-Gazette* article by Cynthia Howell, 4 November 1996, page 1B.

U.S. News and World Report, Vol. 45, October 1958, pp. 73-75.

The Encyclopedia of Arkansas, online at www.encyclopediaofarkansas.net.

(Reprinted with permission from the Little Rock School District.)

Lesson Plans:
Memory Project Interview Guide

How to Make History—in Five Key Questions:
A Quick Guide to Interviews for *The Memory Project*

Overview

As part of this year's Freshman Class, you can help "make history." You don't have to be famous; you just need to ask questions and then listen.

Actually, you'll be helping to make a history website—a kind of *oral history museum*. Your job is to find older people who can tell about personal experiences they had during the changing times of the Civil Rights movement, as well as in later decades or in other countries.

Of course, the story of the Little Rock Nine—the nine African-Americans who attended our school in 1957—is a famous event in all the history books now. But the story in 1957 at Central is just the *first part* of a *much longer* story that historians want to save. And the interview that you do will become part of a permanent education website—called *The Central High Civil Rights Memory Project*.

The changes happened beyond schools, too—in public places, work-places and neighborhoods. And they happened not just in the South, but in every other part of America. Historians want to preserve the stories people can tell about these changes. This "oral history" is an important part of the historical record, but it will disappear soon.

For this special project, you don't have to drag out a long list of questions. You first want to get a few details for contact info and for historical details. Next you can just ask a few *key questions* to trigger some memories, and then you listen and let the stories come out.

Interview Information

Interviewee *(person interviewed)*

Full name _____

Place and date of birth _____

Current occupation _____

Current address _____

Consent signature:

❏ *Yes, I am willing to add this interview to the school's website for*
use by students, teachers and historians:

_____.

❏ *Yes, I am willing but I want the name to be anonymous.*
Use "John Doe"/"Jane Doe."

Interviewer(s)

Name(s) _____

Age/Grade/Teacher _____

Place and Date of Interview _____

Relation to person interviewed _____

Other people present _____

Tape Info *(if you record the interview)*:

Type of recording _____

Length _____

Label/Title _____

Key Questions

If you tape record, just ask and listen. If you're not taping, you can jot down a few notes while you listen—especially for names of people or places or for expressions or words they use in particular stories. Ask follow-up questions about parts of the story that interest you. You can get others to jot down notes, too, or ask extra questions themselves. Add these to your notes, too. Have extra paper in case you need it.

1. How old were you and where were you living when the changes in civil rights started happening? Were you in school, or working, or doing something else?

2. What kinds of changes did you see happening where you lived? Were they happening to you or to someone in your family or to someone else you knew?

3. Do you remember particular events or experiences that have stayed with you? When and where did this happen? What happened—how did it start and how did it end? Who all was involved? Do you remember particular things people said?

4. How did you feel at the time it was happening? What did you do? How did you feel about it later? Have you thought about it much since you've grown older? Would you do anything differently if you could do it over?

5. How did this experience change people you knew? How did it change you? Did it affect any choices you made or any situations you were in later in your life?

Memory Project Taping Dos & Don'ts

Taping Interviews: Top Ten Tips

1. **DO** check your video camera (or tape recorder) *before* you try to use it. Know how to start, pause, rewind and fast forward.

2. **DO** have a blank tape (preferably two!) Have a label on it *before* you start.

3. **DO** have your batteries re-charged—or else bring the external power cord and an extension cord.

4. **DO** find a quiet, comfortable room to do the interview. Make sure there's plenty of light and a place to spread out things if they want to show you letters, clippings, photos, etc.

5. **DO** test the tape *before* you start the actual questions. Say the date and place and your name and then have them say their name. Stop, rewind, and playback the tape to make sure you can see and hear it. Then start recording again at that point.

6. **DON'T** be shy about asking them to repeat something if some noise in the background made it hard to hear.

7. **DON'T** sit far away and try to zoom in with the camera. Instead, sit close (5-10 feet) and use wide-angle. The picture will be steadier, even if you're using a tripod, and the sound will be *much* better.

8. **DON'T** hide behind the camera! If you're filming *and* interviewing, use a tripod. Once you've got them framed in the viewfinder, lean around the camera and listen face-to-face. Better yet, let someone else hold the camera and you ask questions.

9. **DON'T** forget to get their permission to use the tape for our educational website! Be sure they sign the consent line on your Interview Guide or a note you write.

10. **DON'T** forget to say thanks!

[P.S. One extra DON'T: **DON'T** forget to shift the tab on the tape to "Save"!]

Memory Project Book Editors' Reflection

This book of selected essays requires an introduction, literally. Future readers need to know both how and why you chose these particular essays. To help create the Intro, consider your answers to the following questions (and feel free to generate and answer other questions you feel are also relevant.)

Those students who have (1) read all of the essays nominated for the book and (2) complete this reflection assignment will be named as members of the Editing Team in the Credits Page.

Questions

1. What criteria have you used to identify a particular essay as "important for others to read"? What reasons did you use to exclude essays that had been nominated?
2. How are certain essays related to others—in terms of both similarities and differences? What recurring themes have you noticed?
3. In the process of reading the essays, what have you learned about historical events related to civil rights history?
4. What parts of the history seem to be missing, based on your prior knowledge? Which narratives in these essays contradict— or challenge—your prior point of view?
5. What have you learned about the kinds of personal choices that individuals have made when confronted with acts of discrimination—or with acts of reconciliation?
6. What have you learned about the ways in which racism or discrimination is carried on by institutions? What have you learned about the ways the policies of institutions can be changed?
7. What interested you most in these essays? What surprised you most?
8. What questions would you want readers to consider as they read these essays?

Memory Project Book Discussion Questions

You Be the Teacher:
"After Reading These Essays, What Questions Do You Want to Ask Others Who Read the Book?"

Overview

Would you like to help publish a book of oral history about people's experiences during times of Civil Rights struggles? Here's how you can be part of the project:

A total of 60 essays from the Central High Civil Rights *Memory Project* website have been selected by Central High students. The students said these particular essays are "especially important for others to read." They will be published soon in book form. One last chapter needs to be written. This will be a chapter of Discussion Questions for the people who read the book. You are invited to read, reflect and send your questions to the Student Editing Team.

Bonus: Every student who reads at least five of the selected essays and writes at least five discussion questions will be named in the Credits page of the book.

Activity

Get a copy of five of the selected Memory Project essays from your teacher. After you read each essay, think like your English teacher! Identify the key ideas in the essay story. Come up with the "Guiding Question" that could be attached to the essay:
- Write the title of the essay you read.
- Write a few sentences describing your thoughts and reactions to that essay.
- Write a question that would help other readers think about the important idea(s) or the personal life experiences you found in the story.

Flight
Melody Chang

Index of Interviewers, Interviewees, and Other Contributors

Our Free America
Ross Cooper